Building Leadership Competence

A Competency-Based Approach to Building Leadership Ability

Second Edition 2022

ISBN- 9798404629385

Centrestar Learning

State College, Pennsylvania

Building Leadership Competence

"If you are an executive who strives to be within the elite or best-of-class in leadership, Wesley Donahue's book is an essential read for you. Executives leading in today's ever-changing and fast-paced environments must understand which competencies are essential to their success. Wes's book explains in great detail what these 35 competencies are and how to master them. Absolutely a great read!"

- Patricia Macko, Ph.D., MSIT, Organization Development Consultant, Geisinger Health System

"This book is a wealth of practical tools and techniques to round out the leader in all of us. Each of us as leaders has blind spots and this guide helps us to identify these and form actionable strategies to improve. The leadership examples from world leaders, business tycoons, sports, and presidents – and even octopi and orangutans – and the guided exercises work together to make this book a comprehensive, relatable performance improvement resource for individual contributors up through the highest levels of executives."

- John Dolan, Ph.D., Associate Dean, Georgetown University

"Building Leadership Competence is a no nonsense guide that is to the point and provides you with the knowledge, skills, and passion that you need to become a better leader. From beginning to end, Dr. Donahue gives it to you straight: study hard, work to improve, and you will not only become a better employee, but an essential asset to your organization. It's a guide for any leader who wants to become more effective, strategic, operationally focused, and technically competent. It hits all the right core topics, is easy to follow, and had me thinking about my job like I never had before. Provocative, challenging, and a great resource to be the best you can be: highly recommended!"

- Nikhil Juneja, Design Release Engineer – Project Leader, General Motors

"Dr. Donahue's straightforward approach to assessing your aptitude in various leadership skill areas in his book: Building Leadership Competence is direct and insightful. His recommendations on how to build your leadership competence are tactical, providing practical tips that are simple and relevant for today's fast paced workplace. I was able to assess, reflect, and quickly apply the techniques I learned into my daily work. Dr. Donahue has delivered not only a leadership book, but also a resource guide that one can revisit frequently, improving one's leadership skillset over time. Building Leadership Competence is a must read! I highly recommend this book!"

- Danielle Evanoski, Ph.D., Management Consultant Manager, Fortune 500 Consulting Firm.

"This easy-to-use comprehensive guide is an excellent tool for developing the essential-to-success leadership competencies. The self-assessment and structure of the book provide clear goal-focus and make individualization easy. An added bonus is that the development guidelines have application across all levels of leadership and all types of organizations."

- Dr. Katheryn K. Woodley, Industrial-Organizational psychologist; retired Penn State Management Development faculty member with over 30 years of experience in leadership development

Building Leadership Competence

A Competency-Based Approach to Building Leadership Ability

Preface

This book grew out of having been an engineer with interest in developing processes that help people streamline and replicate success and from my work with thousands of people who wanted to become more effective leaders.

I have discussed with many people the interesting question of whether leaders are born or made. My philosophy is that heredity plays a factor in being an outstanding leader, however, all leaders can improve, and especially when they continue to learn, take the time to plan their goals, and have a road map to follow. This book offers a unique and straightforward approach for professionals to assess their leadership skills, develop personalized roadmaps for success, and access on-demand micro-learning courses and other resources that get results. This approach has helped thousands of people achieve success. It will help you too.

Throughout my career, I have appreciated the saying that those who do not learn from the lessons of the past are destined to repeat them. History gives many lessons we can benefit from if we frame and align the lessons to our goals. I included some of these in the book, and used examples from the natural world, to help describe the 35 competencies in the leadership competency model and assessment inventory.

The book is based on sound research and years of experience in a variety of industries and organizations, and from the know-how gained in teaching others how to be successful leaders. Effective leaders achieve success through a combination of learning, planning, and acting.

You too can be an exemplary leader, employee, role model, and visionary. You start by defining what success means to you, assessing your skills, and formulating a plan. People do not always agree on what success means or on how to measure it. Although most agree that it involves a sense of accomplishment, which requires having the knowledge and skills necessary to complete tasks efficiently, professionally, and to the highest standards.

This book supplies the knowledge and practical steps you will need to create the future you want. You will need to provide the grit.

The road ahead is yours: Take it.

Dr. Wesley E. Donahue 2022

Acknowledgements

I did not create this book alone, and I want to acknowledge the people who contributed significantly to the work: Drs. Lisa Donahue and Rebecca Sarnaski for their invaluable research efforts in tracking down articles, books, and other sources needed for identifying examples; Richard Tunaley and Billie Tomlinson for their editing and attention to detail; Valentine Platon for formatting and adding graphics that help bring the text to life; Michael Miller for the custom animal line drawings; Sommoade for the custom people line drawings; Jason Ritter and Alex Donahue for thoughtful design consultation; the individuals who took the time to review the manuscript, and many thousands of people who participated in surveys, focus groups, and interviews, without whom this book would lack the richness of real-world detail. To all these people I offer a sincere and heartfelt Thank you!

Contents

Introduction

Introduction

Welcome!

Do you excel in the knowledge and skills relevant to your career and ambitions? Do you know the competencies you must develop, fine-tune, and express to advance in our competitive world?

If not, you have come to the right place. Armed with the knowledge and tools this guide provides, you will be able to:

- Identify and explore the competencies you want to develop.
- Gain insights and leadership lessons taken from the world's most celebrated leaders as well as from the natural world.
- Make the best use of proven strategies, tips, and resources for advancing your skills.
- Shift your career into high gear.

Working through the material presented here will help you perform at your highest potential on both a personal and organizational level. Do you aspire to move forward in your career? Do you own your own business? Do you want to be a leader in your organization? Do you want to reach the top of your career?

Then this book is for you!

Audience

This book is intended for individuals who want to develop their leadership capabilities. It is a valuable tool for individuals to use in self-assessing their competencies and building their skills by following a systematic and proven approach.

Although the book is directed toward individuals, faculty teaching in university and college leadership programs will also find it useful as a supplementary text to bridge theory and practice.

People who just want to know more about leadership can use the book as a discussion guide in seminars, workshops, and learn-at-lunch programs.

Purpose

This book will help you find the best path forward as you continue your success. How? The book demonstrates that you are the one responsible for your accomplishments and it gives you a competency model to show you the knowledge you need, and a road map to follow as you develop your skills.

The book describes essential 35 Competencies you must have to succeed as an employee, professional, and leader. By working with the 35 Competencies – recognizing why they matter and actively applying what you learn to fine-tune your mastery – you can build the leadership competence needed to excel in your career. Working with the 35 Competencies will also help you become the most effective employee or employer you can be.

Organization

First, be aware that the information in this book is research-based. Over 5,000 business professionals were assessed to validate the leadership competency scale and establish the 5 Competency Clusters and 35 Competencies this book describes.

Resource Management
Competency Cluster

Professional Competence
Competency Cluster

Supervisory Management
Competency Cluster

Organizational Leadership
Competency Cluster

Technical Acumen
Competency Cluster

Competency Cluster A: *Resource Management*

The Resource Management cluster discusses the competencies associated with managing resources. Specifically, we look at computer literacy, technical competence, resource usage, managing resources and projects, and understanding systems.

Competency Cluster B: *Professional Competence*

The Professional Competence cluster describes the critical thinking competency and the various soft skills that all leaders must develop. These include the ability to learn and work with new information, self-management, interpersonal skills, and oral and written communication.

Competency Cluster C: *Supervisory Management*

The Supervisory Management cluster describes the competencies that supervisors must demonstrate, such as coaching, flexibility and resilience, solving problems, decisiveness, conflict management, teamwork, influencing and negotiating, customer/client focus, and relationship building.

Competency Cluster D: *Organizational Leadership*

The Organizational Leadership cluster covers information related to the primary functional areas of almost all organizations. For example, these competencies include human performance management, planning, financial and budgeting essentials, technology management, creative thinking, strategic thinking and planning, and leading change.

Competency Cluster E: *Technical Acumen*

The Technical Acumen cluster explores the specific technical skills an effective leader must have. These include discussions of job-specific technical competencies, occupational competencies, and industry competencies.

SECTION I: PLAN YOUR CAREER

It might not seem like it now, but you are the only person in charge of your career. In this section, you will learn about the value of planning for your professional development and discover a practical framework for developing yourself as a leader. You will learn how to set realistic goals, complete a Leadership Competency Inventory™ (LCI), and create a Competency Action Plan to guide your development.

SECTION II: STUDY THE 5 COMPETENCY CLUSTERS AND THE 35 COMPETENCIES

In Section II, you will study the 35 Competencies that all leaders must demonstrate to be successful in today's world. You will find detailed descriptions, self-assessment questions about your competencies, and resource lists to help you continue learning.

SECTION III: BUILD YOUR COMPETENCE

This section summarizes the book, highlights the salient points, provides an opportunity for you to reflect on your learning, and points the way to your next steps. It is one thing to learn how to do something, but until you apply that knowledge in the real world, you will not know if you have achieved your goals. Further, in today's ever-changing world you are never finished learning. You must continually challenge yourself to stay current in all competencies, or you may lose your competitive edge.

APPENDICES

The appendices provide supplemental information helpful to people using multi-rater feedback systems, and people who want to assess team and group competencies.

Appendix E provides additional Competency Action Plan worksheets.

How to Use this Book

We structured this book to be a hands-on guide with options for how to use the material.

One way to use the book is to read it straight through. Or you can jump to specific sections depending on your interests and goals. Start by reviewing the table of contents, so you understand the organization. Then scan the book. Scanning will help you pinpoint areas where you have an information gap and areas where you may feel confident. From there, you can set your learning goals.

However, for those who want to develop their competencies using a structured and proven approach, we recommend a method for you to follow. It is the most efficient and effective way to improve your competence. We walk you through a research-based road map in **Section I: Plan Your Career**.

In Section I, you start by considering what leadership means to you and writing your goals. Next, you complete the **Leadership Competency Inventory™** (LCI). This will help you identify the clusters that exhibit your top competencies and the first two or three competencies that you need to develop. You will then develop a Competency Action Plan and be ready to study the competencies you want to develop first.

Section II: Study the 5 Competency Clusters and 35 Competencies describes each competency in detail. For your first two or three competencies, you will complete exercises and reflect on how to put what you read into action. You will also find resource lists to assist you in further developing the competencies.

After you finish those first two or three, you can go back and review your **Leadership Competency Inventory™** worksheet and select the next two or three competencies to develop.

Being a dynamic leader involves being a life-long learner, a person who seeks knowledge and who knows how to find the information they need to get the job done. In **Section III: Build on Your Success**, you will find information to guide you in continuing your new habits of planning, learning, and applying what you have learned.

As with most things in life, you will get out of this book only what you put into it. To truly learn and grow you must engage fully with the material presented. Ask yourself questions as you work through the book. Answer the questions that the text asks. Make notes. Look for ideas new to you and consider how they fit with your current knowledge. Recognize what you already know and can build on, and what might be a new way of looking at things.

This book aims to ensure that your skills are at the highest level they can be. Engaging with the book will help you write a better resume, answer interview questions more effectively, be a better employee, move up the corporate ladder faster, and become a more rounded professional who experiences success in your chosen career.

Section I
Plan Your Career

Planning is essential for a successful career. As with any journey, to grow your competencies and ultimately your career, you must define where you want to go and what you will need to know in order to get there.

In this section, we discuss ideas to help you:

- Appreciate that you are the one responsible for planning and developing your career.

- Learn how to plan your goals and manage your time to the best advantage.

- Consider what leadership means to you.

- Realize the importance of core values and how they shape your success.

- Understand what the term competency means and how it is used in business and academic environments.

- Complete a self-assessment that will focus your attention on the competencies you need to develop.

- Create action plans that will guide you as you learn and practice your new skills.

Section 1

You Are in Charge of Your Career

Things don't just happen; they are made to happen.

– John F. Kennedy[1]

As President John F. Kennedy said, for things to happen, one must take action. When that "thing" is your career, it is you who must act. You decide what knowledge, skills, attitudes, and behaviors you want to improve. You work step-by-step to gain the information you need, and not only by reading, but by practicing what you have read.

So how do you ensure success? One important way is by planning. You must identify where your knowledge and skills are weak, and then decide what steps you will take to improve. Success does not come without planning and action. People talk about luck, and certainly a little serendipity helps, but relying on luck is not a plan. To plan means to be proactive.

Consider What Leadership Means to You

Being a leader does not necessarily mean that you aspire to be the CEO of a *Fortune 500* company, though you might! It does not even mean that you must become the president of an organization. Being a leader can mean, of course, being a team leader, a faculty chair, a manager, a supervisor, or any other kind of leader. But being a leader can also mean simply being an excellent employee who takes initiative and serves as a positive role model. Therefore, no matter your role now or what you aspire to become, when we talk about being a leader *we are talking about you*.

Have you heard the saying that those who have not learned the lessons of history are destined to repeat them? It means that by reading and learning about the experiences of others we increase our chances for success, and perhaps without having to experience the same obstacles. This book connects you to examples and resources gleaned from decades of experience, which will help you learn valuable lessons in leadership.

What Must You Know to be Successful?

The elements required for constructing a successful leadership career are: goals and a plan, linked to developing essential competencies of a leader. However, there is no globally accepted agreement on what "competency" means. For purposes of this book, we define competencies as the measurable and observable knowledge, skills, attitudes, and behaviors (KSABs) critical to successful job performance.

No one skill set ensures success, and no universal, agreed upon standard spells out all the specific competencies you must have. Various industries and organizations have their own lists. Universities typically specify entry levels for their programs based on data gathered from industry professionals.

That is why, after years of research – and real-life experience – we have assembled a comprehensive framework of **35 Competencies** that help leaders and professionals like you attain the education and know-how necessary to build successful careers. These wide-ranging competencies are essential for success across virtually every industry, organization, and position.

Each competency discussion in this book gives you what you must know to perform successfully. Each one also provides additional resources for you to continue growing, including books, web links, and courses you can take. But never feel limited by these suggestions. When a competency grabs your interest – or when you feel that you still need to grow in a certain area – conduct your own research and see what ideas you can find and what new lessons you can learn.

Importance of Core Values

Values and Beliefs are at the heart of leadership. While certain competencies are required – and important for leaders to fulfill their roles and meet performance expectations – achieving these are not enough to guarantee effectiveness. At the heart of leadership are the core values and beliefs of an individual and organization.

Values are the codes individuals live by and the codes organizations adhere to as they work to achieve their missions. Values help define who you are, and values help organizations define what they expect from their members. But the values individuals and organizations choose can vary widely.

Consider how your personal and organizational values align with your leadership goals and aspirations, and realize that core values are the base of exemplary performance. What do you value in the workplace, and how important are the following values to you?

- Honesty / Trust / Respect / Human Dignity / People / Fun

- Meaningful Work / Employee Development / Organizational Learning and Agility

- Work Ethic / Positive Attitude / Focus on Success / Delivering Value / Drive for Results

- Quality Products and Services / Effective and Efficient Operations / Innovation

- Safe Working Conditions / Environmental Protection / Customer-Focused Excellence

- Contribution to Society / Global Teamwork / Respect / Adhering to the Law / Ethics and Transparency

When you decide to take a job with an organization, you would be wise to first consider the organization's core values and beliefs and whether they match your own. Then you will be well positioned to plan your pathway to success and choose a framework for leadership development.

Competencies and Performance

The term *competency* has become a buzzword, but that does not make it meaningless. Quite the contrary. Today, competency-based education is said to be the learning of the future. Why? Organizations are discovering that basing decisions on competencies helps them determine what their employees are capable of and where they need to grow.

People sometimes use the term competency without understanding its meaning. In education and in business, *competency* refers to a level of proficiency achieved by a person as measured against a set of standards.

Competencies are the measurable and observable knowledge, skills, attitudes, and behaviors (KSABs) critical to successful job performance. Competencies refer to the specific KSABs that a person can readily show. They include not only technical skills, but also what are known as soft skills.

Many organizations have, or are establishing, formal methods for measuring employee skills. Many now use competency-based assessments to see how prepared, valuable, and successful their employees are. Many also detail such competencies in their job descriptions.

Thus, the level at which a person can demonstrate specific competencies will impact how valuable the person will be to an employer. Additionally, some universities now use competency demonstration, rather than grades, to show that their students are professionally prepared.

By assessing your current skill level in each competency, and by creating an action plan to improve where needed, you will become a better employee, a more effective leader, and a more successful person.

Take Control of Your Career by Writing Goals

Productivity is never an accident. It is always the result of a commitment to excellence, intelligent planning, and focused effort.

– Paul J. Meyer[2]

Successful careers are built on two things: a list of goals and a plan. Think about where you are in life and ask yourself if you are on a trajectory toward success.

Before you start looking at where you are and what you need to learn, take a step back and decide what success means to you. What we mean is that you must assign an attribute – a specific goal – to the concept of success, and then you can evaluate whether you have achieved success in that goal.

Without goals you cannot know if or when you have achieved what you set out to do; and you cannot know when you are finished and ready to move to the next goal. Without specific goals, you will not know if you have succeeded.

You must not only have goals. You must have SMART goals.

If you read any management or leadership book or search online for "goals in leadership," you will not get far before you discover information on SMART goals. Here is what you will learn:

- A <u>S</u>MART goal is *specific.*

- A S<u>M</u>ART goal is *measurable.*

- A SM<u>A</u>RT goal is *attainable.*

- A SMA<u>R</u>T goal is *relevant* and *realistic.*

- A SMAR<u>T</u> goal is *timely.*

Planning your time is a significant part of life, both in and out of work. What are your priorities today; over the next six months; long term? The point is this: If you truly want to accomplish anything, including building your leadership competence, you must set goals. Then, you must plan how you will achieve those goals.

Accomplishing your short-term goals requires that you develop daily and weekly plans to better control the way you use time. Even short-term plans need to be SMART.

On the other hand, understanding long-term planning can literally change your life. Typically, you will achieve short-term goals between today and up to a year from now. Long-term goals are goals that will take longer than one year to accomplish.

You must write your long-term goals. Thinking about goals is not enough. Further, you must write them as SMART goals. Start by listing at least one long-term leadership development goal you want to achieve. Then, beneath each goal, write at least two short-term plans or actions you will take to help you achieve that goal.

LONG-TERM GOAL 1 _____

Short-term actions: _____

_____

_____

_____

LONG-TERM GOAL 2: _____

Short-term actions: _____

_____

_____

LONG-TERM GOAL 3: _____

Short-term actions: _____

_____

_____

_____

As we now know, to have a successful career you need two things: goals and a plan. But you also need a third thing: skills.

As mentioned previously, you will not find a globally accepted list of talents, on competencies, that every employee and leader should have.

Next, you will assess your skill and knowledge levels using the Leadership Competency Inventory™. You will use your self-assessment results to create your Competency Action Plans.

Assess Your Competencies Using the Leadership Competency Inventory™

The **Leadership Competency Inventory**™ (LCI) and the associated Competency Action Plan worksheet are based on extensive research in both the private and public sectors. The competencies in the LCI have been identified as important for successful performance in multiple leadership roles at various organizational levels and in many industries.

For purposes of the LCI, a competency is a set of skills, knowledge, attitudes, and behaviors that are observable and measurable, and that contribute to excellent performance in a specific job or role.

Note: LCI is a self-assessment approach that identifies training and development needs of both individuals and groups. The focus in this book is on individual self-assessment and development. If you are working with a multi-rater system or with a team or larger group, see the Appendices for information on how to use the LCI for these activities.

Define Your Job Responsibilities

Start your self-assessment by defining the target, which in this case is your job. In other words, when you answer the self-assessment questions in the Leadership Competency Inventory™, you will do so by thinking about your job performance and respond accordingly.

Start by completing the Job Responsibilities worksheet, below. It will help you clarify what is important in your job. List the responsibilities, activities, or decisions that are most typical of your job and that occupy most of your time. Describe the most critical responsibilities or complex activities that your job requires. To increase the accuracy of your LCI, provide as much detail as possible.

Job Responsibilities Worksheet

Name: _____ Date: _____

Organization: _____

Job Title: _____

What responsibilities, activities, and decisions are required in your job? Please provide five examples:

1. _____
_____

2. _____
_____

3. _____
_____

4. _____
_____

5. _____
_____

What are the most complex activities or decisions that are critical to meeting your job responsibilities? Please give five examples:

1. _____
_____

2. _____
_____

3. _____
_____

4. _____
_____

5. _____
_____

Complete the Leadership Competency Inventory™ (LCI) Worksheet

Now you are ready to assess your skills using the LCI worksheet.

Read the description for each competency question and quickly rate the importance and the development need that each one has for you. As you make your ratings, consider the activities and decisions you listed as representative of your job.

The two ratings are different and independent of each other. Importance indicates how vital that competency is in meeting the responsibilities associated with your job. Development Need indicates how much you think you need to develop that competency.

Rate them both using a 5-point scale, with **1 being the lowest** and **5 the highest**. An individual competency can be high on both importance and development need, low on both, or high on one and low on the other.

Here is an example:

COMPETENCY	IMPORTANCE (I)	DEVELOPMENT NEED (DN)	VALUE (I x DN)
1. **Computer and Basic Literacy** – proficient in using personal computers and learning new software; reads, writes, and performs mathematical operations; speaks and listens with comprehension	1 2 3 4 ⑤	1 2 ③ 4 5	

COMPETENCY	IMPORTANCE (I)		DEVELOPMENT NEED (DN)		VALUE (I x DN)
	LOW HIGH		LOW HIGH		
1. **Computer and Basic Literacy** – proficient in using personal computers and learning new software; reads, writes, and performs mathematical operations; speaks and listens with comprehension	1 2 3 4 5		1 2 3 4 5		
2. **Technical Competence** – works with various technologies as required for the job	1 2 3 4 5		1 2 3 4 5		
3. **Resource Usage** – identifies, organizes, uses, and allocates resources	1 2 3 4 5		1 2 3 4 5		
4. **Resource Management** – demonstrates awareness of technical resources; knows how to apply resources to achieve desired outcomes	1 2 3 4 5		1 2 3 4 5		
5. **Understand Systems** – grasps complex interrelationships and interdependencies	1 2 3 4 5		1 2 3 4 5		
6. **Conceptual Thinking** – thinks creatively, can visualize concepts; uses reasoning to make decisions and solve problems	1 2 3 4 5		1 2 3 4 5		
7. **Learning and Information** – demonstrates ability to develop new awareness, knowledge and skills; acquires and uses information productively	1 2 3 4 5		1 2 3 4 5		
8. **Self-Responsibility and Management** – displays responsibility, self-confidence, emotional self-control, integrity and honesty	1 2 3 4 5		1 2 3 4 5		
9. **Interpersonal Skills** – appropriately sociable, interacts effectively with others	1 2 3 4 5		1 2 3 4 5		
10. **Oral Communication** – makes clear and effective oral presentations to individuals and groups; listens to others	1 2 3 4 5		1 2 3 4 5		
11. **Written Communication** – communicates effectively in writing; can critically review and comprehend information written by others	1 2 3 4 5		1 2 3 4 5		
12. **Leadership and Coaching** – models and encourages high standards of ethical behavior; adapts leadership styles to situations and people; empowers, motivates, guides, and coaches	1 2 3 4 5		1 2 3 4 5		
13. **Flexibility and Resilience** – adapts to change in the work environment; effectively copes with stress and ambiguity	1 2 3 4 5		1 2 3 4 5		
14. **Problem Solving** – recognizes and defines problems; analyzes relevant information; encourages alternative solutions and plans to solve problems	1 2 3 4 5		1 2 3 4 5		
15. **Decisiveness** – decides and responds quickly and makes difficult decisions when necessary	1 2 3 4 5		1 2 3 4 5		
16. **Self-Direction** – realistically assesses strengths and weaknesses; invests in self-development; demonstrates self-confidence; can work persistently toward a goal; manages time effectively	1 2 3 4 5		1 2 3 4 5		
17. **Conflict Management** – anticipates and seeks to resolve disagreements, complaints and confrontations in a constructive manner	1 2 3 4 5		1 2 3 4 5		
18. **Teamwork and Cooperation** – demonstrates and fosters cooperation, communication and consensus among individuals and groups	1 2 3 4 5		1 2 3 4 5		
19. **Influencing and Negotiating** – keeps key groups and individuals informed; appropriately uses negotiation, persuasion and authority in working with others to achieve goals; builds productive networks	1 2 3 4 5		1 2 3 4 5		
20. **Customer Focus** – actively seeks customer input; ensures that customer needs are met; continually works to improve the quality of services, products and processes	1 2 3 4 5		1 2 3 4 5		

COMPETENCY	IMPORTANCE (I)	DEVELOPMENT NEED (DN)	VALUE (I x DN)
	LOW HIGH	LOW HIGH	
21. **Interpersonal Relationship Building** – considers and responds appropriately to the needs, feelings and capabilities of others; seeks feedback and accurately assesses impact on others; provides helpful feedback; builds trust with others	1 2 3 4 5	1 2 3 4 5	
22. **Human Performance Management** – ensures effective systems for employee selection, placement, development, performance appraisal, recognition and disciplinary action; promotes positive labor relations and employee well-being	1 2 3 4 5	1 2 3 4 5	
23. **Planning and Evaluation** – establishes policies, guidelines, plans and priorities; plans and coordinates with others; aligns required resources; monitors progress and evaluates outcomes; improves organizational efficiency and effectiveness	1 2 3 4 5	1 2 3 4 5	
24. **Financial Management and Budgeting** – understands budget process; prepares and justifies budgets; monitors expenses; manages profit/loss ratios as appropriate	1 2 3 4 5	1 2 3 4 5	
25. **Technology Management** – stays informed and applies new technologies to organizational needs; ensures staff is trained and can use technology required for the job	1 2 3 4 5	1 2 3 4 5	
26. **Creative Thinking** – develops new insights and novel solutions; embraces innovations and fosters innovative thinking in others	1 2 3 4 5	1 2 3 4 5	
27. **Vision** – creates a shared vision of the organization; promotes broad ownership	1 2 3 4 5	1 2 3 4 5	
28. **External Awareness** – stays informed on policies, priorities, trends and special interests and uses this information in making decisions; considers external impact of statements, decisions, and actions	1 2 3 4 5	1 2 3 4 5	
29. **Strategic Thinking and Planning** – advocates and participates in strategic planning to define and achieve organizational goals	1 2 3 4 5	1 2 3 4 5	
30. **Management Controls** – ensures the integrity of the organization's processes; promotes ethical and effective practices	1 2 3 4 5	1 2 3 4 5	
31. **Diverse Workforce** – recognizes the value of cultural, ethnic, gender, and other individual differences; provides employment and development opportunities for a diverse workforce	1 2 3 4 5	1 2 3 4 5	
32. **Leading Change** – leads organizational transformation and change efforts; champions organizational change	1 2 3 4 5	1 2 3 4 5	
33. **Job-Specific Technical Competencies** – demonstrates knowledge, skills, and ability and uses proper methods and procedures to successfully perform job responsibilities specific to current job (such as bank teller, patient access representative, machine operator, benefits specialist) within an organization or work group	1 2 3 4 5	1 2 3 4 5	
34. **Occupational Technical Competencies** – demonstrates knowledge, skills, and abilities needed within current occupation (such as engineer, HR professional, lawyer, nurse) and stays current with relevant occupational changes and developments	1 2 3 4 5	1 2 3 4 5	
35. **Industry-Wide Technical Competencies** – demonstrates knowledge, skills, and abilities needed within the industry (such as manufacturing, hospitality, financial services, education, healthcare, transportation) and stays current with relevant industry changes and developments	1 2 3 4 5	1 2 3 4 5	

Identify the Top Ten Competencies You Want to Develop

Now that you have assessed your skills and rated yourself as to importance and development need, you can calculate a value for each competency. You do that by multiplying your importance and development need scores. You will use your value scores to compare all the competencies, which will help you identify the competencies that are your top priorities for development.

Write the calculated score in the Value column. Here is an example:

COMPETENCY	IMPORTANCE (I)	DEVELOPMENT NEED (DN)	VALUE (I x DN)
1. **Computer and Basic Literacy** – proficient in using personal computers and learning new software; reads, writes, and performs mathematical operations; speaks and listens with comprehension	1 2 3 4 ⑤	1 2 ③ 4 5	15

Once you have calculated a value for all the competencies, review the value scores on your answer sheet and put a check next to the top ten. *These are the competencies that are most important to you and that have the highest development need.*

Now, consider how these top ten competencies relate to each other. The Centrestar Leadership Competency Model™, below, groups the competencies into five clusters.

Using the values from your LCI, check the ten competencies in which you had the highest values. For example, assume your Computer and Basic Literacy value score is 15 and that it is one of your highest scores. You would then check "1. Computer and Literacy Skills" on the Centrestar Leadership Competency Model™ chart below. Continue until you have checked your ten highest scores.

Centrestar Leadership Competency Model™

D. Organizational Leadership

_____ 22. Human Performance Management
_____ 23. Planning and Evaluation
_____ 24. Financial Management and Budgeting
_____ 25. Technology Management
_____ 26. Creative Thinking
_____ 27. Vision
_____ 28. External Awareness
_____ 29. Strategic Thinking and Planning
_____ 30. Management Controls
_____ 31. Managing Diverse Workforce
_____ 32. Leading Change

E. Technical Acumen

_____ 33. Job-Specific Technical Competencies
_____ 34. Occupational Technical Competencies
_____ 35. Industry-Wide Technical Competencies

B. Professional Competence

_____ 6. Conceptual Thinking Skills
_____ 7. Learning and Information Skills
_____ 8. Self Responsibility and Management
_____ 9. Interpersonal Competence
_____ 10. Oral Communication
_____ 11. Written Communication

A. Resource Management

_____ 1. Computer and Basic Literacy Skills
_____ 2. Technical Competence
_____ 3. Resource Usage
_____ 4. Resource Management
_____ 5. Understands Systems

C. Supervisory Management

_____ 12. Leadership and Coaching
_____ 13. Flexiblility and Resilence
_____ 14. Problem Solving
_____ 15. Decisivness
_____ 16. Self Direction
_____ 17. Conflict Management
_____ 18. Teamwork and Cooperation
_____ 19. Influencing and Negotiating
_____ 20. Customer Focus
_____ 21. Interpersonal Relationship Building

After you check your top ten competencies on the Centrestar Leadership Competency Model™, examine the pattern of your checks and answer the following questions:

1. What five competency clusters do most of your "top ten" (high-value competencies) fall into?

_____

_____

_____

2. What insights do the relationships among your high-value competencies give you? How might these insights help you plan the actions you want to take to develop your skills?

_____

_____

_____

Based on your insights and interests, select **two** or **three competencies** you want to develop right now.

Here is a word of caution. While it is exciting to see the results of your self-assessment and understand what competencies to focus attention on, be aware that growth is a process that needs time and attention. For that reason, we advise you to focus on no more than two or three competencies at any one time. Limiting your focus is the most efficient way to make progress. If you try to take on too much at one time you may become overwhelmed and that will not serve your purpose.

Later, after you are satisfied that you have learned what you need to know about those first few competencies, you can return to the Centrestar Leadership Competency Model™ and repeat the process by picking the **next** two or three competencies you want to develop.

By following this approach, you will make a long-term commitment to continually developing the skills most associated with success in your position. If you should get a new position, follow this same approach to identify and develop the competencies you must have to be successful in that position.

This is the most effective, streamlined, and enjoyable method of building competence no matter what your situation.

Kickstart Your Growth with Competency Action Plans

Now you are ready to use the **Competency Action Plan worksheet**, below, to crystalize and record the actions you want to take to develop the two or three competencies you have selected.

Using the worksheet, you will think about how improving your performance in the competency will assist you in your job, and you will identify the resources and people who can help you learn. To stimulate your thinking, you can read more about the competencies in Section II: Study the 5 Competency Clusters and the 35 Competencies, where each competency is described in detail.

Note: You will find some blank worksheets in Appendix E. It may be useful to photocopy the worksheet, especially if you plan to develop other competencies later.

Competency Action Plan Worksheet

Competency: _____

Briefly describe how improvement in this competency will help you achieve important results or better meet your job responsibilities.

_____

_____

_____

List courses, books, or independent study opportunities that could help you develop this competency.

_____

_____

_____

Identify one or more people who could help you, either as a role model or source of information. Write any questions you would like to ask each person.

_____

_____

_____

What specific steps will you take?	Start Date	Finished

Completing the worksheet is an excellent planning step.

Now the development work begins. You are ready to dive in and learn the things you need to know to be successful.

In Section II: Study the 5 Competency Clusters and the 35 Competencies, we focus on developing the competencies, which involves learning about and locating the information you need and building your skills.

Grow your abilities, your character, your education, and your capacity. You can decide who you want to be and get about the business of becoming that person.

– Dave Ramsey[3]

Section II
Study the 5 Competency Clusters and the 35 Competencies

Competencies are the measurable and observable knowledge, skills, attitudes, and behaviors that make or break job performance. For our purpose, competency refers to the level of proficiency that you as an employee can demonstrate as measured against a set of standards. In other words, competencies matter because they are how employers will judge your work.

In this section, we describe the 35 competencies that leaders across all industries are expected to demonstrate. For each competency, you will find ideas to help you:

- Understand what the competency looks like in the workplace, and realize the specific observable and measurable knowledge, skills, attitudes, and behaviors involved.

- Recognize the value of the competency from reading about how the competency is seen in nature. You will appreciate that competencies are universal facts of life.

- Realize that exceptional leaders have faced the same kinds of problems you face and that you can learn from their attitudes and behavior.

- Self-assess your current performance, which will pinpoint where you need to improve.

- Get specific action steps you can use right now, today, by reviewing the "what to do" suggestions. Focusing on these actions is a great way to continue growing your skills.

- Appreciate that while you may feel alone in your daily struggle to excel, many resources are available to you. By exploring a list of appropriate resources, you will find something to help you grow.

- Reflect on what you learned, which will help you own it.

Competency Cluster A:
Resource Management

*If you get stuck, draw with a different pen.
Change your tools; it may free your thinking.*

– Paul Arden[4]

Resource management is the first competency cluster we will consider. No matter how intelligent, educated, or well-trained you are, there is always more to learn. Even the wisest leader needs to continually assess the resources requirements of his work group, identify appropriate resources to meet current needs, use resources efficiently, and manage the planning and implementation of new resources as needed.

Here we describe the competencies you need to manage resources and projects successfully. These are: **computer and basic literacy**, **technical competence**, **resource usage**, **resource management**, and **understanding systems**.

As you read, consider your own experience managing resources. Ask yourself questions such as: Do I know what resources are available? Do I understand how to properly use resources? Do I have a resource deficit? Do I know when to seek new resources? Do I know how to fill any gaps in my knowledge?

If you have a printed copy of this text (an excellent strategy!) take notes in the margin as you read. Highlight what you feel is important and what you want to remember. Note any questions you want to research or resources that you will review later.

COMPETENCY 1
Computer and Basic Literacy

IMPORTANCE (I)	DEVELOPMENT NEED (DN)	VALUE (I x DN)
1 2 3 4 5	1 2 3 4 5	

Proficient in using personal computers and learning new software; reads, writes and performs mathematical operations; speaks and listens with comprehension.

I think it's fair to say that personal computers have become the most empowering tool we've ever created. They're tools of communication, they're tools of creativity, and they can be shaped by their user.

– Bill Gates[5]

The new millennium is often called the Information Age. That is because ideas and information move around the globe faster than ever before. Some say that the dawn of computers means that humans rarely must interact with each other, but this is not true. In fact, if you search online about how much people communicate, via technology, you will find much research regarding concerns about the demise of interpersonal communication. But, after 2012, writing on the topic slowed down, probably because people realized we do not communicate and write less than we used to; we just do it differently. Writing and communicating is just as important as it has always been, perhaps more so. We are always using technology to communicate our ideas in written, graphic, video, and audio forms.

Computer literacy and general communication skills are essential for every professional, at any stage in your career. Simply put, you must know how to use computers, know your way around software commonly used in business and in your field, and understand the basics of the Internet and social media. You must know how to perform basic mathematical computations, have good speaking and listening skills, possess solid writing skills, and have the drive to learn new software skills as necessary. This is why our first competency targets Computer and Basic Literacy.

1

To clarify the concepts applicable to this competency, read the following list of observable and measurable knowledge, skills, tasks, and behaviors that are essential to all professionals, no matter what organization:

- ✓ **Computer Literacy** – uses computers and technology efficiently; operates computers and understands the language used in working with a specific system or systems.

- ✓ **Reading** – locates, understands, and interprets written information presented in documents such as manuals, graphs, and schedules.

- ✓ **Writing** – communicates thoughts, ideas, information, and messages in writing; creates documents such as letters, directions, manuals, reports, graphs, and flow charts.

- ✓ **Arithmetic and Mathematics** – performs basic computations and approaches practical problems by choosing appropriately from a variety of mathematical techniques.

- ✓ **Listening** – receives, attends to, interprets, and responds to verbal messages and other cues.

- ✓ **Speaking** – organizes ideas and communicates effectively when talking to individuals and groups.

Leadership Learning:
Computer and Basic Literacy

The Nature of Leadership

Dogs focus on the basic literacy skills of listening and responding and this has helped them become known as man's best friend.

When it comes to listening and responding to verbal messages, nothing beats a well-trained dog. We all know the focus that a canine companion possesses. Dogs watch their owners with eyes wide and tails wagging, ready to leap to action when a message is sent, and ignoring anyone except their special human.

Well-trained dogs that love their owners will listen, respond, and attend to the smallest verbal and non-verbal clues. They will also sit on their person's lap when the human is sad, seeming to commiserate and offer nothing but affection. Research shows that dogs sense human anger and fear, and even read our expressions, from despair to happiness. Dogs express themselves in simple and straight forward ways: You always know what a dog is thinking.

Humans, too, need this type of empathy and clarity to be effective in their communication. A good leader senses when something is wrong in their team. This does not require a sixth sense, or the amazing nose of a canine. It requires only that the leader pays attention to team members, asks questions, is present, and acts when necessary.

An effective leader is compassionate and understanding when necessary, and firm and clear when needed. A good leader sniffs out trouble, just like a dog might do, and is as in tune with the emotions of those they work with as a well-trained police dog.

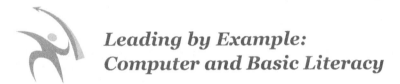

Leading by Example: Computer and Basic Literacy

Real Life Leaders

Steve Jobs was a major force behind computers and computer literacy.

1

Steve Jobs, co-founder of Apple, seems both an obvious choice as an example of a leader exemplifying computer skills. Surely Jobs was beyond computer literate, right? True, but what made Jobs an amazing leader and visionary was his understanding that computer technology is the beginning of competence, not the end.

Jobs said, "It is in Apple's DNA that technology alone is not enough – it's technology married with liberal arts, married with the humanities, that yields us the results that make our heart sing" (as quoted in Lehrer, 2011).

Jobs continually demonstrated his belief that computer technology was a vehicle to help people communicate, learn, interact, and grow. He knew how to marry his understanding of format, style, and design, like that inherent in calligraphy, to modern computers (Lehrer, 2011). He knew how to excite people by facilitating communication. Jobs was a computer and communication visionary who led his company to the pinnacle of interpersonal communication and computer technology.

Assess Your Skills: Computer and Basic Literacy

Take a moment to consider what you know about this concept and assess your skills. Indicate your level of agreement with each question.

How competent am I	Very little	Somewhat	Very much
Do I have the necessary computer skills to do my work?			
Do I know how to conduct research on the internet and find sources that support my ideas or help me to revise my position?			
Am I able to adapt to new software, hardware, and technologies?			
Do I have a basic understanding of social media platforms and how they fit with my job, organization, and industry?			
Do I understand how to write concise yet effective texts, tweets, emails, and documents?			
Is my writing is clear, easy to read, and effective?			
Do I have the basic mathematical skills necessary to understand my work and make good decisions?			
Is computer and basic literacy an area where I am skilled?			

7 Tips – What To Do:
Computer and Basic Literacy

The following tips will help you how to become more successful and continually improve your competence in this area. Check those that you need to develop.

- [ ] 1. Make a list of all the computer and basic literacy challenges you face. Rewrite each challenge to be an objective. List several ways to reach each objective.

- [ ] 2. Find others in your organization who have the computer skills or knowledge you lack. Ask to observe, work with, and get feedback from them.

- [ ] 3. Separate the computer and technology skills you do have from those you do not have and structure your development to gain expertise in the areas where you are lacking.

- [ ] 4. Identify those individuals that use social media appropriately and ask them to mentor you.

- [ ] 5. Ask open-ended questions that require more than yes or no answers.

- [ ] 6. Before responding via email, text, or tweet take a moment to reflect on the content and how others might react. Give yourself time to formulate appropriate responses.

- [ ] 7. Ask a trusted friend to evaluate your email, text and tweeting habits and suggest ways you can improve.

Development Plan Resources:
Computer and Basic Literacy

Perhaps you think your skills are adequate in this competency. It is easy to believe if you have had a long career in business or you are an active participant in the Information Age, and you may well be competent in business and technology. However, there is always more to learn about computers, technology, and basic literacy and communication.

Build your expertise by reviewing the sources listed below:

1

Learning and Development Resources

Centrestar Academy. *Business Writing Styles and Business Writing Grammar.* www.centrestar.com

Chenier, N.J. (2005). *Chenier's practical math application guide: For do-it-yourselfers, trades people, students, etc.*

Kahn Academy. *Free basic computer and other tutorials.* Visit www. khanacademy.org

Snarski, R.D. (2018). *Communicating clearly in the information age.*

Wilson, G. (2020). *Beginners guide to computer literacy: A well written guide on the computer basics, component, shortcuts and its uses.*

The best idea is meaningless unless when you present it other people rally around.

Reflection and Application: Computer and Basic Literacy

Whether you sell pharmaceuticals or manage a *Fortune 500* company, you must have certain basic skills to be effective and competitive in today's world. You must have basic computer skills and be able to operate rudimentary technology such as computers, smart phones, printers, and so forth. You must also have effective communication skills. This means knowing how to talk to people and how to write, for example, emails, texts, social media postings, and evaluations.

Remember:

- Everyone in the workforce needs to use basic computer and Internet technology.

- Even if you do not use technology in your job now, a time will come when you need those skills. For example, you may need to apply for a new position or a government grant, research your competitors, or price-check supply purchases.

- To stay current, you must constantly reassess your computer, math, and communications skills.

1

The most important concept I learned about this competency is:

_____

_____

_____

_____

_____

_____

_____

_____

_____

_____

_____

_____

_____

_____

_____

_____

_____

_____

_____

_____

_____

_____

_____

_____

_____

_____

1   To effectively apply this concept to my development I plan to:

_____

_____

_____

_____

_____

_____

_____

_____

_____

_____

_____

_____

_____

_____

_____

_____

_____

_____

Do not become a dinosaur! Basic computer and communication skills will serve you well in any job, at any level.

2

COMPETENCY 2
Technical Competence

IMPORTANCE (I)	DEVELOPMENT NEED (DN)	VALUE (I x DN)
1 2 3 4 5	1 2 3 4 5	

Proficient in selecting technology and tools, applying technology to a task, and maintaining and troubleshooting technology.

The number one benefit of information technology is that it empowers people to do what they want to do.

– Steve Ballmer[6]

Having basic computer, writing, and communication skills is important, however, to truly excel you must have insights and practice beyond basic literacy. You must assess your technical competence, which is your ability to work with the various technologies that are required to not only do your job but to do it efficiently and effectively.

Often as a leader you will be called upon to understand, consider, and even authorize the purchase of technologies that are, perhaps, outside your area of expertise. Therefore, you must understand tools, equipment, technology, and procedures at a level sufficient to help you make effective decisions.

To clarify the concepts applicable to this competency, read the following list of observable and measurable knowledge, skills, tasks, and behaviors essential to all professionals:

- ✓ ***Selects technology*** – appropriately chooses procedures, tools, and equipment.

- ✓ ***Applies technology to task*** – understands overall intent and proper procedures for set up and operation of equipment.

- ✓ ***Maintains and troubleshoots equipment*** – monitors, investigates, and resolves problems related to equipment.

*Leadership Learning:
Technical Competence*

The Nature of Leadership

Some suggest that our ability to use tools separates us from the animals– that, and our opposable thumbs. The truth is, while opposable thumbs are rare in the animal kingdom, they do exist. In fact, a variety of primates have opposable thumbs, as do some species of marsupials, the giant panda, and even the maned, or crested, rat in Africa. So, we must refute the possession of opposable thumbs as distinguishing us from animals. But what about the use of tools as an ability that makes us special? Sea otters bang shells on rocks to open them; some primates poke sticks into holes looking for bugs; and elephants use twigs to swat away insects (Choi, 2009). An even more interesting example is the discovery that octopuses use tools to take cover from danger.

Octopi are master escape artists who are inventive, and they display technical competence.

Scientists have learned that the octopus is an intelligent creature, with some suggesting it is among the most intelligent of creatures. Proof of the armed sucker's intelligence comes from observing their use of tools. Divers have seen octopus using coconut halves as shelter (Kaplan, 2009). They were observed not simply to find a coconut shell and dash under it in a time of danger. Rather, the octopus has been observed to find a coconut shell and then carry it around just in case it needs it (Kaplan, 2009). In other words, they identify a problem and make a plan to solve it, pick their tool, and hold on to the tool for a rainy day.

What is so amazing is that the octopus understands that danger may come from anywhere at any time; most animals do. What is more, the octopus knows that while it could outrun the danger in many situations, having a plan to hide could be a life-saving alternative. The octopus plans ahead of a problem! It knows that a ready hiding spot is not always available, so when it encounters a transportable one, it has the forethought to bring it along.

The octopus anecdote is applicable to your leadership success in that you must anticipate future needs and prepare to meet them. This entails being aware of your technological surroundings, including your overall industry, knowing what technological tools are at your disposal, and knowing how and when to use them.

Leading by Example:
Technical Competence

Real Life Leaders

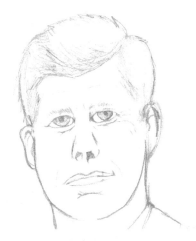

John. F. Kennedy was the first major politician to effectively use of TV to reach people.

President John F. Kennedy was a great communicator, and he also understood how he could use technology to deliver his message. Kennedy was the first U.S. President to effectively employ television to communicate directly with the American people. A few presidents before him had appeared on television, but they were not aware of how to capitalize on the opportunities television provided.

Using his natural looks, charm, and wit, Kennedy became beloved by a nation through the charisma he exuded in his televised speeches. He realized this technology was the future, so he learned how to use it. He worked on his televised persona, and he won an election and the hearts of people by communicating in a way that exuded confidence and authority. He was, by choice, one of the first properly televised leaders, as well as being a forward-thinking person.

Assess Your Skills:
Technical Competence

Take a moment to consider what you know about this concept and assess your skills.
Indicate your level of agreement with each question.

How competent am I	Very little	Somewhat	Very much
Am I computer literate and comfortable with my technology skills?			
Do I have the knowledge and experience to select the proper tools and equipment in my workplace?			
Do I know how to troubleshoot technology issues and where to turn for help?			
Do I know what resources I have to ensure that I use technology appropriately?			
Do I take the necessary actions to stay informed, current, and adept at managing the technologies in my workplace?			

7 Tips – What To Do:
Technical Competence

The following tips will help you to become more successful and continually improve your competence in this area. Check the competencies you need to develop.

☐ 1. Keep a log of the technical questions and problems that arise in your environment and that people ask about. To help determine your strengths and weaknesses, analyze the list to identify situations where you have skills and where you are lacking.

☐ 2. Find others in your organization who possess the skills or knowledge you are weak in. Ask to observe, work with, and get feedback from them.

☐ 3. Try to become the expert in your organization in one or more technical areas. Then encourage colleagues to use you as a sounding board for their technical ideas.

☐ 4. Identify what you do know as opposed to what you do not know and structure your work unit to provide technical expertise in areas where you are lacking.

2

☐ 5. Attend training classes or professional courses to ensure proficiency in your technical areas of responsibility.

☐ 6. Network with other professionals in your field. Become aware of emerging technological advances that could impact your field. Keep current on technical literature and developments. Share relevant technical articles among members of your work unit.

☐ 7. Foster a climate of continual learning in your work group by drawing on the expertise of your colleagues and having them share their knowledge through demonstrations, presentations, and written papers.

Development Plan Resources: Technical Competence

Build your expertise by reviewing the sources listed below:

Learning and Development Resources
Centrestar Academy. *Creating a Culture of Continuous Improvement.* www.centrestar.com
Mantle, M. W. and Lichty, R. (2020). *Managing the unmanageable: Rules, tools, and insights for managing software people and teams.*
Stokes, A. (2015). *Is this thing on? A friendly guide to everything digital for newbies, technophobes, and the kicking & screaming*
Wempen, F. (2015). *Digital literacy for dummies.*

Individuals and organizations either get better or worse, excellence requires a culture of continuous improvement.

2

Reflection and Application: Technical Competence

Managing technology involves more than just understanding technology. It also involves being a champion for necessary changes in equipment and technology. It also requires being willing and capable of supporting other technology users.

Remember:

- As a leader you must not only know how to use the tools that you employ every day, but also how to prepare for, evaluate, select, and implement technology throughout your workplace.

- Employees and leaders must know the basic trouble-shooting procedures for the technology they work with, and where to go for assistance when needed.

The most important concept I learned about this competency is:

_____

_____

_____

_____

_____

To effectively apply this concept to my personal development I plan to:

_____

_____

_____

_____

_____

_____

Understand the technology around you and know where to go for assistance.

COMPETENCY 3
Resource Usage

IMPORTANCE (I)	DEVELOPMENT NEED (DN)	VALUE (I x DN)
1 2 3 4 5	1 2 3 4 5	

Effectively identifies, organizes, uses, and allocates resources.

The most dangerous kind of waste is the waste we do not recognize.

- Shigeo Shingo[7]

Getting a job done right involves effectively using the resources available to you, such as allocating your time wisely, being alert to deadlines, and proactively accomplishing your goals. It can also mean preparing budgets, organizing computer files, communicating results, and finding resources.

The types of resources you may need might seem endless. The trick is to not only use resources that are given to you, but to also determine what other resources might improve the overall process and job results.

To clarify the concepts applicable to this competency, read the following list of observable and measurable knowledge, skills, tasks, and behaviors essential to all professionals:

- ✓ **Time** – selects goal-relevant activities, ranks them, allocates time, and prepares and follows schedules.

- ✓ **Money** – uses or prepares budgets, makes forecasts, keeps records, and makes adjustments to meet objectives.

- ✓ **Materials and Facilities** – acquires, stores, allocates, and uses materials and space efficiently.

- ✓ **Human Resources** – assesses skills and distributes work accordingly, evaluates performance and provides feedback.

Leadership Learning:
Resource Usage

3

The Nature of Leadership

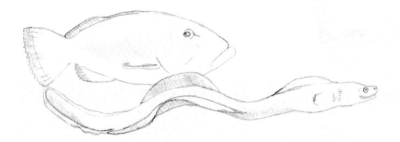

Groupers use moray eels as a resource by teaming up with them to create a cooperative and efficient hunting team.

The large but regal grouper uses resources effectively.

When a grouper is hunting and its prey goes into hiding, the grouper will look around to spot a large giant moray eel. The grouper attracts the attention of the eel by vigorously shaking its body in a way that directs the moray eel to the hiding prey. This effective use of resources turns the grouper and moray eel into a cooperative and efficient hunting team.

The grouper knows how to use its speed to chase prey. But it also knows that sometimes it can use the sleek, muscular body of the moray eel to flush prey from their small hiding places into the open, where the speed of the grouper can be put to better use. In the absence of a moray eel, the grouper reevaluates its resources and may similarly team up with the large hump head wrasse fish whose jaws can suck prey from cracks and crevices.

Knowing how to use its own resources, such as speed, to chase prey, can help keep a grouper fed. But this intelligent fish knows that sometimes it must use its body as a resource, shimmying and head-shaking to bring the new resources of the moral eel or hump head wrasse to bare on the situation and get a good meal for all participants. People can learn from the grouper how to identify what resources can work best in what situation, and then organize and allocate resources to accomplish every task on a to-do list.

Leading by Example: Resource Usage

Real Life Leaders

Clara Barton excelled at organizing groups.

Although void of such a lofty ambition when she first set out, Clara Barton was destined to be the founder of the American Red Cross. In fact, in 1860, she had no way of knowing that she would create such a profound legacy a hundred and fifty years into the future and would positively impact the lives of millions.

A ground breaker from the start, Barton was the first woman to open a free government school and the first woman to hold a position as a patent clerk. Then, the American Civil War banged on Barton's door and changed her life.

She quickly became involved in the war, directly caring for the injured. A natural leader, Barton learned how to effectively use the resources she had available. As it became increasingly difficult to keep up with the carnage, Barton led the way to a better system of care. She created the practice of triage, separating patients via the seriousness of their injuries. She also organized committees of women to find organizations that would donate medical supplies, a resource which makeshift hospitals were sorely lacking. Barton's amazing leadership helped her garner the nickname, "Angel of the Battlefield."

She went on to found the American Red Cross in 1881, and established protocols for helping victims of natural and man-made disasters. She served as the organization's president for more than twenty-three years. Thanks in no small part to her amazing leadership and creative use of resources, today the American Red Cross still serves during emergencies and is one the world's best-known humanitarian organizations.

Assess Your Skills: Resource Usage

Take a moment to consider what you know about this concept and assess your skills. Indicate your level of agreement with each question.

How competent am I	Very little	Somewhat	Very much
Do I know what resources are available to me?			
Do I know how to find and use new resources?			
Do I effectively manage my time?			
Do I understand the value of budgeting, forecasting, and other financial tasks?			
Do I manage materials and facilities effectively?			
Are my human resources skills up to par?			
Do I share resources effectively with others?			
Am I am open to suggestions from others about resources?			

7 Tips – What To Do: Resource Usage

The following tips will help you how to become more successful and continually improve your competence in this area. Check those that you need to develop.

☐ 1. List all the resource usage challenges facing you. Rewrite each challenge as an objective. List several ways to reach each objective.

☐ 2. Keep a log of the resource usage questions and problems that others ask you for assistance with. Analyze how you were able to help them to determine what your strengths and weaknesses are.

3. Find others in your organization who are adept at identifying, organizing, planning, and allocating resources. Ask to observe, work with, and get feedback from them.

4. Draw on the talents of your work unit or peers in making resource usage judgments.

5. Separate in your mind what you know from what you do not know. Structure your work unit to provide resource usage expertise in areas where you are lacking.

6. Attend training classes or professional development courses in project management.

7. Collaborate with your colleagues in establishing realistic project plans and performance expectations. Discuss and obtain a detailed understanding of the usage requirements for projects.

Development Plan Resources: Resource Usage

Build your expertise by reviewing the sources listed below:

Learning and Development Resources
Centrestar Academy. *Managing Time and Multiple Priorities.* www.centrestar.com
Delaney, D. (2013). *New business networking: How to effectively grow your business networks using on-line and off-line methods.*
Gavin, P. (2021). *The workplace guide to time management: Best practices to maximize productivity.*
Sarder, R. (2011). *Learning: Steps to becoming a passionate lifelong learner.*

The hours of the day are the only resource we all have in equal number. Remember, how you spend your time is how you live your life!

Reflection and Application: Resource Usage

3

Review the resources allocated for a project and evaluate whether they are adequate. If they are, determine how you can best leverage them. If they are not, look for alternative – or supplementary – resources.

Remember:

- On a challenging or large-scale project, identify the resources most needed.

- Plan and organize how to procure and use a specific resource. If you are uncertain, ask someone who is knowledgeable.

- Learn for the future by tracking what resources were most useful to you and identify the ones you may want to use or replace in future projects.

- Consider how technology could be an effective resource, perhaps by using a new software system or technical tool that you may not have considered previously.

The most important concept I learned about this competency is:

_____

_____

_____

_____

To effectively apply this concept to my personal development I plan to:

_____

_____

_____

_____

_____

_____

The ability to use resources wisely is a sign of an effective leader.

COMPETENCY 4
Resource Management

4

IMPORTANCE (I)	DEVELOPMENT NEED (DN)	VALUE (I x DN)
1 2 3 4 5	1 2 3 4 5	

Demonstrates awareness of technical resources; knows how to effectively apply resources to achieve desired outcomes.

The key is not to prioritize what's on your schedule, but to schedule your priorities.

- Stephen Covey[8]

Projects require numerous inputs to get the job done. One might need a team of workers, materials, money, and other resources necessary to deliver on time, within budget, and successfully. Of course, you always need to manage time and workloads. In short, there is always some type of resource that not only needs to be used, but that also needs to be managed to accomplish the goals your organization expects of you.

A good supervisor knows how to manage resources – time, money, employees, facilities – to get the job done right. This might include setting schedules, figuring out budgets, or even delegating these tasks to others, but in one way or another, you must constantly manage resources.

To clarify the concepts applicable to this competency read the following list of observable and measurable knowledge, skills, tasks, and behaviors essential to all professionals:

✓ Demonstrates technical proficiency and accuracy in areas of responsibility.

✓ Understands and considers the resources and technical difficulty and complexity placed on colleagues, stakeholders, and others by the nature of their work and resource usage.

✓ Appropriately applies procedures, requirements, regulations, and policies related to specialized areas of expertise.

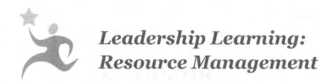

Leadership Learning: Resource Management

4 **The Nature of Leadership**

Parrots use beauty and brains to manage resources well.

Parrots come in all shapes, sizes, and colors, but one thing they have in common is that almost all species are good problem solvers who know how to manage their resources.

Parrots have intrigued humans for centuries by mimicking our speech. In captivity, these birds can learn to use that speech to ask for treats and gain attention. But parrots can do much more than simply mimic sound.

These intriguing avians maintain a keen awareness of their surroundings and of the technical resources available to them. Many parrots learn, without training, how to achieve a desired outcome – reaching food or freedom – by manipulating cage latches and puzzles, and even using tools. Parrots can use sticks to open cage latches or solve food puzzles, and can even learn to forage for their resources, knowing that a tool they need may be hidden from plain view.

Whether in the wild or in captivity, parrots know what they need and want, and they

have the adaptability to manage their resources to get it. In fact, kea birds, a mountain parrot endemic to New Zealand, have been known to rip apart cars in an effort to get at the food inside. These small but intelligent birds have earned a reputation for mischief in the island nation, but also for creative thinking and effective – if destructive – resource management.

Just as parrots bring their surprisingly agile brains to bare on situations, people need to be aware of what technical resources they have at their disposal, and how best to use these resources to achieve a desired outcome. We may have advanced beyond using a stick to free a piece of food from a box, as many parrots and other birds do when solving puzzle boxes, but we can take a page from their playbook by learning to be aware, adaptive, and creative in how we use our technical resources.

Leading by Example: Resource Management

Real Life Leaders

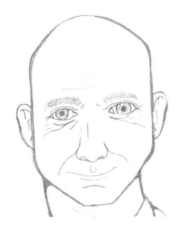

Jeff Bezos is a resource management leader through his use of innovative contracts to bring value to customers.

Jeff Bezos knows how to manage resources. He has done so very effectively since opening a small online bookstore and using his mother's garage to store inventory. Bezos believes in understanding the market, and in using your knowledge and resources to your advantage.

As the founder of Amazon.com, Bezos learned that customers wanted books delivered quickly and at the best prices. He merged this understanding with a large product catalog and an amazing distribution system, and subsequently led Amazon to become one of the most well-known and profitable companies in the world.

Bezos' secret lies in understanding his customers – obsessing over them even – and giving them what they crave. He believes in providing wide selections and lower prices, along with fast and reliable delivery. He established innovative contracts with various shipping carriers, including the U.S. Postal Service for Sunday delivery, which helped him meet his goals.

Assess Your Skills: Resource Management

Take a moment to consider what you know about this concept and assess your skills. Indicate your level of agreement with each question.

How competent am I	Very little	Somewhat	Very much
Do I understand the resources my staff needs to do their jobs?			
Am I confident my staff has the necessary resources and that they know where to find them?			
Do I understand my organization's policies and procedures?			
I Do I know what resource challenges are facing me?			
Do I know what resource challenges are facing my work unit?			
Do I know what resource challenges are facing my organization?			
Do I effectively use others on my team as resources?			
Do I place a high enough priority on collaboration and teamwork?			

7 Tips – What To Do: Resource Management

The following tips will help you become more successful and continually improve your competence in this area. Check those that you need to develop.

- [ ] 1. List all the resource management challenges facing you.

- [ ] 2. Keep a log of the resource management questions and problems that others ask you for assistance with. Analyze what you were able to help with.

☐ 3. Keep a list of relevant technical resources and share relevant information among members of your work unit.

☐ 4. Network with other professionals in your field. Be aware of emerging technological advances that could impact your field.

☐ 5. Continually update your knowledge of policies and regulations that apply to your area of technical expertise and ensure all projects accommodate the requirements.

☐ 6. Take a project management course or find others in your organization who are good at managing projects and resources.

☐ 7. Maintain proficiency in your area of expertise by keeping up with technical literature and developments. Draw on the talents of your work unit or peers to help in making resource management judgments.

Development Plan Resources: Resource Management

Build your expertise by reviewing the sources listed below:

Learning and Development Resources
Centrestar Academy. *Understanding Project Management Tools.* www.centrestar.com
Mantle, M.W. & Lichty, R. (2019). *Managing the unmanageable: Rules, tools and insights for managing software people and teams.*
Moriarty, T. (2019). *The Productive Leadership™ system: Maximizing organizational reliability*
Weise, M. (2020). *Long life learning: Preparing for jobs that don't even exist yet.*

The critical first 10 percent of project management is project planning.

Reflection and Application: Resource Management

People and money are obvious resources to consider and manage. But also think about resources such as time, computer access, data, access to people with knowledge, and so forth.

Remember:

- On a challenging or large-scale project, list the resources you must manage.

- Empower your team members to manage the resources they are using.

- Keep your team informed. Make sure that if something happens to one member you have a back-up who can fill in and keep the project going.

- Work with your leadership or team to brainstorm new resources that may be helpful or best practices for using existing resources.

The most important concept I learned about this competency is:

_____

_____

_____

_____

To effectively apply this concept to my personal development I plan to:

_____

_____

_____

_____

_____

_____

Well trained, enthusiastic employees are one of your greatest resources.

COMPETENCY 5
Understand Systems

IMPORTANCE (I)	DEVELOPMENT NEED (DN)	VALUE (I x DN)
1 2 3 4 5	1 2 3 4 5	

Grasps complex interrelationships and interdependencies.

What's important is that you have a faith in people, that they're basically good and smart, and if you give them tools, they'll do wonderful things with them.

– Steve Jobs[9]

Nothing exists in a vacuum. To understand, for example, why a child throws repeated temper tantrums one often must look to the parents and their parenting style, as well as the child's health and natural demeanor. To see why a product is not working one must look at the instructions, the user, the design – the entire system.

A good manager understands how systems work together to get something done. They know that when there is a problem in one part of the system other areas could be negatively impacted. The ability to see the entire forest, as well as the trees, is paramount.

To clarify the concepts applicable to this competency read the following list of observable and measurable knowledge, skills, tasks, and behaviors essential to all professionals:

✓ **Systems Orientation** – knows how social, organizational, and technological systems work and operates them effectively.

✓ **Monitors and corrects Performance** – distinguishes trends, predicts impacts on system operations, diagnoses system performance, and corrects malfunctions.

✓ **Improves or Designs Systems** – suggests modifications to existing systems and develops new or alternative systems to improve performance.

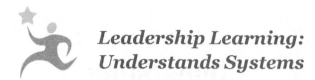

Leadership Learning: Understands Systems

The Nature of Leadership

Hermit crabs, anemones, and bristle worms use shells as a system.

An effective leader is a person who understands how systems work together. This means not having a singular view of just your system, but seeing the big picture, understanding how one resource impacts another. In nature, the hermit crab does this commendably.

Hermit crabs and bristle worms are sea creatures who may sometimes live alone, but at other times come together in a unique symbiotic relationship. Those who do not understand this system may think that the worm or anemone is a parasite, but that is not correct. To appreciate this marine triad, you must understand the entire system.

The hermit crab needs a shell to survive. In an excellent example of resource management, the hermit crab combs the ocean floor looking for a shell of just the right size to live in. But its management skills do not end there. The hermit crab will sometimes find that a bristle worm is trying to resource the same shell. Rather than being affronted at this apparent home invasion, the hermit crab recognizes it as an opportunity.

You see, the bristle worm eats dead, decaying flesh, an unwanted waste product that might otherwise get stuck in the hermit crab's shell and becoming a problem. So, the hermit crab allows the bristle worm to live under the protection of its shell in exchange for this cleaning service.

But the cooperation does not end there.

Sometimes, an anemone will make its way onto the top of the hermit crab's shell, attach itself, and take up residence. But this little blob does not live rent free. The presence of the anemone helps keep the hermit crab safe. Many sea creatures that might be tempted to dip into the shell to grab a crab snack think twice when faced with the stinging tentacles of the anemone.

So, what you have is a group of three creatures who live together, offering each other food and protection. They become a system, which makes them much more effective than their individual parts.

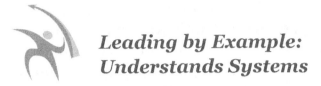

Leading by Example: Understands Systems

Real Life Leaders

Jackie Robinson understood systems and used them to change the world.

Developing and nurturing relationships can be difficult, particularly when those relationships are complex. But cultivating rapport with people who differ from us socially, economically, religiously, ethnically, and in various other ways not only helps us grow as individuals but gives us a greater understanding of the world around us.

One of the most impactful figures in exemplifying complex interrelationships is baseball legend Jackie Robinson. Most recognize Robinson as the first African American to play Major League Baseball (MLB), putting an end to the segregation that had permeated MLB since its inception. However, what many people don't know is that he was also the first black MLB television analyst, as well as the first black vice president for a large American organization (Nathan, 2017).

From serving in the military, to being the lone African American man in MLB, to helping run a major corporation, Jackie Robinson was quite adept at handling the complexities of relationships, not just as a human but as a black man breaking barriers at a time when many people were fighting to keep those barriers intact. His

5

calm demeanor and determination helped the American civil rights movement gain traction.

Despite being treated poorly throughout his career (both in baseball and the corporate realm), Robinson persevered. Although well-known for his reluctance towards interdependence, Robinson was quite aware of his impact, and the path his trailblazing paved for others. While he was not particularly concerned with the opinions of others, he realized the importance of fostering significant relationships. Robinson proved that regardless of whether others want you to succeed, how you continue to move forward is all that matters.

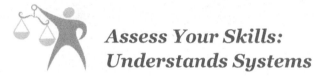

Assess Your Skills: Understands Systems

Take a moment to consider what you know about this concept and assess your skills. Indicate your level of agreement with each question.

How competent am I	Very little	Somewhat	Very much
Do I understand how the social systems work in my organization?			
Do I understand the technological systems in my workplace?			
Am I prepared to monitor and correct performance issues?			
Do I regularly evaluate the processes and systems in my area?			
Do I assess problems and make improvements to systems?			
Do I understand trends in my industry?			

7 Tips – What To Do:
Understands Systems

The following tips will help you become more successful and continually improve your competence in this area. Check those that you need to develop.

☐ 1. Examine and benchmark the performance of best-in-class work units to understand what methods, processes, and systems contribute to their success.

☐ 2. Evaluate the methods, processes, and systems of other units to see how your unit compares, and to see what you can learn from others.

☐ 3. Develop standards of work-unit performance and communicate them to your colleagues.

☐ 4. Understand the trends and technological factors that affect or might affect your organization and its methods, processes, and systems. Stay abreast of trends by reading technical journals and magazines related to your area of expertise.

☐ 5. Formulate an improvement plan by defining goals and objectives, designing the systems in a way to achieve the goals and objectives, assigning responsibilities, allocating resources, and being aware of potential problems.

☐ 6. Encourage colleagues to use you as a sounding board for ideas related to improving performance.

☐ 7. Draw on the talents of your work unit or colleagues to help grasp the complex interrelationships and interdependencies related to your organization's methods, procedures, and systems.

Development Plan Resources: Understands Systems

5

Build your expertise by reviewing the sources listed below:

Learning and Development Resources
Centrestar Academy. *Controlling Projects to Completion.* <u>www.centrestar.com</u>
Brown, J. (2012). *Systems thinking strategy: The new way to understand your business and drive performance.*
Brynteson, R. (2010). *Once upon a complex time: Using stories to understand systems.*
Meadows, D. (2021). *Summary and analysis of thinking in systems: A primer.*

Some claim that emotional intelligence, and knowing what is going on around you, is more important than your IQ.

Reflection and Application: Understands Systems

The world looks very different from space than it does if you stand in the middle of a rain forest, or in the middle of Central Park. From space, you see an entire system. Close up, you see individual parts. Both views are essential.

As you consider how well you understand systems, remember:

- A team is only as strong as its weakest link.

- When something is not going right, look at the big picture to see where the problem is, or if some secondary problem is influencing things.

- Training is important in every organization. A well-designed training program prepares people for their jobs and increases their enthusiasm, which makes the entire system run better.

- Planning is perhaps the most important part of any project.

The most important concept I learned about this competency is:

_____

_____

_____

_____

_____

_____

_____

_____

_____

_____

_____

_____

_____

_____

_____

_____

_____

_____

_____

_____

_____

_____

_____

To effectively apply this concept to my development I plan to:

5

_____

_____

_____

_____

_____

_____

_____

_____

_____

_____

_____

_____

_____

_____

_____

_____

_____

_____

_____

Learn to see the big picture

Competency Cluster B:
Professional Competence

Property is an intellectual production. The game requires coolness, right reasoning, promptness, and patience in the players.

– Ralph Waldo Emerson[10]

In this cluster we cover six areas that relate to professional competence. To be a leader, or even a more effective employee, you must be competent in some basic but significant areas. Competence refers to how well you know how to do your specific job, how well you can find answers to questions that inevitably arise on the job, how well you manage your time and your energy, and how well you communicate with others.

Demonstrating professional competence makes you more effective in your position. It also makes you appear to be credible, helping you become a resource to other people. It makes you feel good about your accomplishments and encourages others to trust you with important tasks. When you are professionally competent you are more likely to have a satisfying career.

Here we describe specific areas of professional competence including: **conceptual thinking**, l**earning and information**, **self-responsibility** and **management**, **interpersonal competence**, **oral communication**, and **written communication**.

COMPETENCY 6
Conceptual Thinking

6

IMPORTANCE (I)	DEVELOPMENT NEED (DN)	VALUE (I x DN)
1 2 3 4 5	1 2 3 4 5	

Thinks creatively and can visualize concepts; uses reasoning to make decisions and solve problems.

In selling as in medicine, prescription before diagnosis is malpractice.

– Tony Alesandra[11]

One dictionary definition of conceptual is "concerned with the definitions or relations of the concepts of some field of enquiry rather than with the facts" (Dictionary.com, n.d.). When one engages in conceptual thinking they strive to "perceive and imagine, predict and hypothesize, and to conclude and reflect" (Jarrard, 2012).

Conceptual thinking is about looking at how things are connected, how they interrelate with other things, so that you can better plan for the future (Jarrard, 2012). As one author put it, "Conceptual thinkers are fascinated by concepts, ideas, relationships, and philosophies. They ask lots of questions and deliberately think things through" (Jarrard, 2012).

To clarify the concepts applicable to this competency, read the following list of observable and measurable knowledge, skills, tasks, and behaviors essential to all professionals:

- ✓ **Creative Thinking** – generates new ideas.

- ✓ **Decision making** – specifies goals and constraints, generates alternatives, considers risks, and evaluates and chooses best alternative.

- ✓ **Problem Solving** – recognizes problems and devises and implements plan of action.

- ✓ **Sensing** – organizes and processes symbols, pictures, graphs, objects, and other information.

✓ **Learning** – uses efficient learning techniques to acquire and apply new knowledge and skills.

✓ **Reasoning** – discovers a rule or principle underlying the relationship between two or more objects and applies it when solving a problem.

6

Leadership Learning:
Conceptual Thinking

The Nature of Leadership

Orangutans understand the concept of the future, think about it, and make plans for it.

Zoos and aquariums usually strive to give animals educational enrichments, things that make their lives better and more interesting and that keep their brains and bodies active. At the Lowry Park Zoo in Florida, a couple times a year, the orangutans are given enrichment packages made by preschool students. These packages often consist of an empty cereal box filled with various treats and then wrapped up in a human shirt, which the primates love to wear and play with.

When the time comes, the oldest, largest male orangutan sees the keeper coming with the packages and moves quickly to the front-most rock ledge, ready to receive a package. He has been around the block a few times and knows how delightful these packages are. He reaches and catches the first package that the keeper tosses out.

As the keeper moves on, the other orangutans catch their packages and promptly open them, eating the peanut butter and other treats inside, or putting on the clothing contained in the package. But not the big alpha male. He hurriedly puts his unopened package behind his back, hiding it from view, then reaches out his arm, asking for another package, almost as if pretending that he never received one. This big guy wants everything he can get. And usually his plan – his attempt at deception – works and he ends up with a second package.

This is an example of conceptual thinking. The large orangutan delays his gratification, hides his package from view, and tries to get more. Once he sees that the keepers are finished handing out packages, the male grabs his creatively, if ill-gotten, loot and heads off to a corner to enjoy.

While this is not to suggest that leaders lie, the orangutan's behavior demonstrates the value of creative thinking, problem solving, and learning and reasoning – all very necessary skills in any leader.

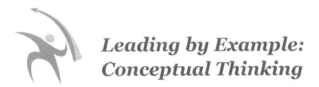

Leading by Example: Conceptual Thinking

Real Life Leaders

Nancy Lubin, one of Forbes 50 Greatest World Leaders, started "Dress for Success."

Not exactly a household name, Nancy Lublin made the 2014 Forbes list of the top 50 greatest world leaders. How? She knew how to think creatively, establish goals, solve problems, and make new things happen. In 1995, Lublin used just $5,000 to start a non-profit organization that lives on more than 25 years later. This organization, Dress for Success, empowers women to achieve economic success by supporting them in various way, one of which is business wardrobe advice.

Lublin became CEO of the failing social change organization Do Something, helping pull it back from the edge of failure and turning it into a thriving organization that has inspired millions of young people to become socially active in more than 130 countries around the globe.

Lublin understands how to creatively use her education and tenacity, and how to bring together technology and people to get things done. Lublin has gone on to write a monthly motivational column, conduct Ted Talks, publish books, and win awards.

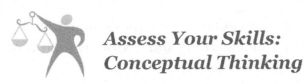

Assess Your Skills: Conceptual Thinking

Take a moment to consider what you know about this concept and assess your skills. Indicate your level of agreement with each question.

How competent am I	Very little	Somewhat	Very much
Am I a creative thinker?			
Do I know how to create effective goals?			
Do I recognize problems before they get out of control?			
Am I proactive in solving problems?			
Do I visualize the elements of complicated concepts and problems?			
Do I typically look at problems from multiple angles?			
Do I take time to think creatively and conceptually, reflecting on the situations around me?			
Do I invite input from others in an authentic way?			

7 Tips – What To Do:
Conceptual Thinking

The following tips will help you become more successful and continually improve your competence in this area. Check those that you need to develop.

☐ 1. Before you try to solve a problem, identify the data you need to reach a solution and how that data can best be obtained.

☐ 2. Before reaching a decision, ensure that all involved agree on the problem definition, then invite contributions from others, and be willing to listen and discuss their ideas.

☐ 3. Look at issues and problems from all possible angles. Make a list of alternatives and consider multiple-decision alternatives, including the worst-case scenario for each decision.

☐ 4. Think about how to use resources, the environment, and organization or industry conditions to your advantage.

☐ 5. Practice brainstorming and ensure there is no judgment or criticism. Record every idea and take a break before evaluating them.

☐ 6. Make a habit of thinking outside the box. Look for novel and nontraditional solutions.

☐ 7. Allot time for thinking, wondering, and experimenting.

Development Plan Resources: Conceptual Thinking

Build your expertise by reviewing the sources listed below:

6

Learning and Development Resources
Centrestar Academy. *Identifying and implementing improvement initiatives.* www.centrestar.com
Baggini, J. & Fosl, P. (2020). *A philosopher's toolkit: A compendium of philosophical concepts and methods.*
Page, S. (2018). *The model thinker: What you need to know to make data work for you.*
Pink, D. (2018). *A whole new mind: Why right-brainers will rule the future.*

When people put their brain power together, they know more and can do more.

Reflection and Application: Conceptual Thinking

Conceptual thinking is not only about looking at the big picture, but also at how the various parts of that picture work together. It is imperative that a good leader exercise conceptual thinking to see relationships between various aspects of a process or project, whether it be teammates, resources, plans, ideas, and all the other inputs that paint the picture being analyzed.

Remember:

- Conceptual thinking is about relationships.
- When using conceptual thinking you need to imagine the possibilities, reflect on what you know, and imagine new possibilities.

The most important concept I learned about this competency is:

6

To effectively apply this concept to my personal development I plan to:

6

_____

_____

_____

_____

_____

_____

_____

_____

_____

_____

_____

_____

_____

_____

_____

_____

_____

_____

_____

_____

Conceptual thinking can involve thinking outside the box.
It is the ability to take an overall view of things and to search for
new meanings and approaches.

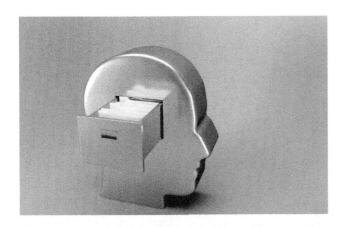

COMPETENCY 7
Learning and Information

IMPORTANCE (I)	DEVELOPMENT NEED (DN)	VALUE (I x DN)
1 2 3 4 5	1 2 3 4 5	

Demonstrates ability to develop new awareness, knowledge, and skills; acquires and uses information productively.

Nobody can make you feel inferior without your consent.

– Eleanor Roosevelt[12]

Entrepreneur Richard Branson, founder of the Virgin Group, talks about the importance of learning and being open to ideas. He says, "I've always been a lifelong learner, interested in discovering how things work, and the people I work with tend to be similar" (2013). Technology, competition, and knowledge are growing and changing today as never before, and the effective leader must change and grow as well.

A few decades ago one could graduate from college informed in a specific area, and work in that field for years without having to challenge themselves to learn new things. Today this approach is ineffective. Every employee, in every field, must learn new things almost every day. From new computer systems to new methods of communication, we all must be lifelong learners.

To better understand the ideas applicable to this competency read the following list of observable and measurable knowledge, skills, tasks, and behaviors essential to all professionals:

✓ Acquires and evaluates information.

✓ Organizes and maintains information.

✓ Interprets and communicates information.

✓ Uses computers to obtain and process information.

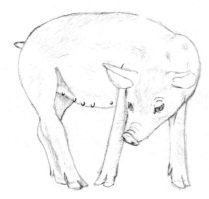

Leadership Learning: Learning and Information

The Nature of Leadership

7

Pigs, perhaps the smartest domestic animals, understand emotions and learn tasks quickly.

When we think of animals that display outstanding learning and information retention, most of us typically defer to rats and mice, as those are among the creatures most commonly associated with research studies regarding cognitive functionality. However, recent findings in biobehavioral research shown that pigs have a tremendous capacity for learning and retention. Not only are they adept at acquiring new skills, but they have impressive olfactory senses (think truffle hunting), and extraordinary emotional aptitude. In addition, (not unlike most humans) pigs have taste preferences, significantly favoring sweet flavors to bitter or sour (Gieling, Nordquist, & van der Staay, 2011).

Also, similarly to humans, pigs have unique personalities and can experience and express a wide range of emotions. In addition, pigs can rank "important" recollections according to significance, a highly valued trait when snuffing out some of the world's most sought-after delicacies, truffles, as opposed to the less desirable run-of-the-mill fungi. They can also recall where they previously discovered the prized tubers and return to collect the edible treasures on command.

Much like their human counterparts, pigs are social animals, and can read and react to the temperaments and behaviors of their fellow swine. They also take social cues when being introduced to a new passel. For instance, if the team has become accustomed to being fed at a certain time, it does not take long for the new members to eagerly anticipate sustenance and prepare according.

While being referred to as a "pig" typically carries with it negative connotations, there is much we can learn from these amazing creatures: learning to prioritize our memories to achieve greater success and happiness; adapting more easily to new surroundings and individuals; discovering valuable information, and continuing to seek out additional data are all traits modeled by pigs, and useful in everyday situations, as humans.

Leading by Example: Learning and Information

7

Real Life Leaders

Susan Wojcicki led by example in showing the world how to use, combine, and communicate information.

YouTube CEO Susan Wojcicki began her climb to success as one of the first 20 people employed by the then small-time organization Google. A true technology leader, Wojcicki envisioned a bright future for YouTube and lobbied Google to purchase the video sharing website, a wise decision, as its value has climbed to more than 90 billion dollars. Google paid just 1.5 billion to acquire it.

As of 2017, Wojcicki was CEO of YouTube. In 2015, Time magazine named Wojcicki, "The most important person in advertising," a title she has earned time and again, most notably by helping YouTube develop and refine its strategy for making money (and millionaires) through advertising.

Like most effective leaders, Wojcicki knows how to use information, how to combine information with current trends, and how to keep an eye to the future when making strategic decisions for the organizations she leads.

Assess Your Skills:
Learning and Information

Take a moment to consider what you know about this concept and assess your skills. Indicate your level of agreement with each question.

7

How competent am I	Very little	Somewhat	Very much
Do I value learning?			
Do I typically know how to find the information needed in any given situation?			
Do I try to be a life-long learner?			
Am I good at organizing information?			
Am I skilled at interpreting and communicating information?			
Do I try to learn something new every day?			
Do I use a variety of sources to make evidence-based decisions in the workplace?			
Do I keep current in my professional field, work, and industry?			

7 Tips – What To Do:
Learning and Information

The following tips will help you become more successful and continually improve your competence in this area. Check those that you need to develop.

☐ 1. Identify the essential learning and information acquisition sources (such as co-workers, news reports, trade journals) that you and others in your organization use.

☐ 2. Find those in your organization who develop new awareness and use information productively. Ask them what they do to acquire information and get feedback from them.

3. Remember that you learn more while listening than while talking. Listen to others and try and understand their points of view. Ask open-ended questions that require more than a yes or no answer.

4. Make a habit of thinking outside the box. Look for novel and nontraditional solutions.

5. Use interviews, observation, and surveys to pinpoint the areas where you want to acquire information, knowledge, and skills.

6. When people in your work unit discuss or debate ideas, require that they explain and substantiate their positions with background information and facts.

7. Keep current through reading about emerging economic, legal, and technological changes and other issues that could impact your organization.

Development Plan Resources: Learning and Information

Build your expertise by reviewing the sources listed below:

Learning and Development Resources
Centrestar Academy. *Analyzing problems.* www.centrestar.com
Chaffee, J. (2018). *Thinking critically.*
Pearse, M. & Dunwoody, M. (2013). *Learning that never ends.*
Sarder, R. (2011). *Learning: Steps to becoming a passionate lifelong learner.*

The organization with the best-trained and educated people will produce the best products and services.

Reflection and Application:
Learning and Information

Lifelong learning is about voluntarily learning new things, reflecting on new insights, and considering how what you are hearing, seeing, and experiencing fits into what you already know. It is also about understanding what other people think and feel, and how your ideas and theirs can coexist. When you open yourself to learning every day, you live a life that is more satisfying, and you also become a better leader.

Remember:

- Encourage those you lead to always be learning and growing. Ensure they have a career path that encourages such growth.

- Remember that learning does not have to mean changing how you think. It can be about simply understanding what other people think.

- You can learn by taking a course, by reading journals and websites, by talking to other people, and by taking the time to reflect on your experiences.

The most important concept I learned about this competency is:

_____

_____

_____

_____

To effectively apply this concept to my personal development I plan to:

_____

_____

_____

_____

_____

Even Einstein never stopped learning.

COMPETENCY 8
Self-Responsibility and Management

IMPORTANCE (I)	DEVELOPMENT NEED (DN)	VALUE (I x DN)
1 2 3 4 5	1 2 3 4 5	

Displays responsibility, self-confidence, emotional self-control, integrity, and honesty.

Management is doing things right; leadership is doing the right things.

— Peter Drucker[13]

Psychologists say that before you can love another person you must be able to love yourself. In a way, the same is true of management: before you can effectively manage other people, you must be able to manage yourself. A person who is disorganized, dishonest, unethical, or unsociable cannot be a good leader.

Leadership and effective supervisory skills are dependent upon certain qualities and abilities relating to controlling your own thoughts and behaviors. An effective manager does not just talk to people, but also listens and understands those they lead. An effective supervisor does not just tell people what to do, but rather knows how to – and continually does – set a good example. A true leader is ethical, kind, cautious, and exhibits self-discipline.

To clarify the concepts applicable to this competency read the following list of observable and measurable knowledge, skills, tasks, and behaviors essential to all professionals:

✓ **Responsibility** – exerts a high level of effort and perseveres toward goal attainment.

✓ **Self Esteem** – believes in self-worth and maintains a positive view of self.

✓ **Sociability** – demonstrates understanding, friendliness, adaptability, empathy, and politeness in group settings.

✓ **Self-Management** – assesses self accurately, sets personal goals, and monitors progress.

✓ **Integrity / Honesty** – chooses ethical courses of action.

Leadership Learning:
Self-Responsibility and Management

The Nature of Leadership

Manta rays exhibit emotional control and self-management.

We all know that humans are social animals, and that wolves, primates, cows, sheep, and elephants are also socially inclined. But did you know that manta rays – the large, soaring creatures of the sea – are also exceptionally social creatures? Mirror self-recognition tests show they even have the capacity to be self-aware and are highly self-confident creatures.

Manta rays can live up to 50 years. Part of this long lifespan can be attributed to the fact that while they are often solitary creatures, they come together and form groups of 50 or more to feed, mate, and migrate. By choosing to interact with other manta rays in the best interest of their squadron, they display a tremendous responsibility and integrity. They have also been known to show a preference for certain other manta rays and to shun particular members of their group (Perryman, et al., 2019).

This scenario is familiar to most of us. In nearly every aspect of our lives where we interact with others, we humans show a proclivity for cliques. This is natural; we tend to gravitate toward those with whom we share interests. While this behavior is understandable, we must be honest with ourselves and others, and especially with people outside our immediate circle. Like manta rays, we must put forth our best efforts toward acting in the best interest of the greater good, while also preserving our integrity and maintaining control of our emotions.

Leading by Example: Self-Responsibility and Management

Real Life Leaders

Nelson Mandela was a mindful leader adept at managing his emotions and inspiring others.

If Nelson Mandela's leadership achievements could be summed up in one sentence it might be what the ceremonial speaker said as Nelson received his Nobel Peace Prize in 1993, "For [his] work for the peaceful termination of the apartheid regime, and for laying the foundations for a new democratic South Africa."

Mandela was a master of self-responsibility and self-management, a confident man who was forgiving and inspiring. Mandela believed in leading from behind, not by pushing people ahead but by allowing people to move ahead and celebrating with them the victories they achieved. He was a mindful leader, adept at understanding and managing his own emotions, and lifting others into the light.

Mandela said, "One of the most difficult things is not to change society — but to change yourself." His was a never-ending quest to improve himself, and in doing so he improved humanity. His leadership traits and values are certainly something we can all aspire to.

Assess Your Skills: Self-Responsibility and Management

Take a moment to consider what you know about this concept and assess your skills. Indicate your level of agreement with each question.

How competent am I	Very little	Somewhat	Very much
Do I consider myself a responsible person?			
Am I proactive and always take initiative?			
Do I value my own skills and self-worth?			
Do I set personal goals that are important and achievable?			
Do I work consistently toward attaining my goals?			
Am I honest and do I act with integrity?			
Do I have a daily "to-do" list where I prioritize what I need to accomplish? Do I stick to it?			
Do I schedule my daily activities effectively?			

7 Tips – What To Do: Self-Responsibility and Management

The following tips will help you become more successful and continually improve your competence in this area. Check those that you need to develop.

- [ ] 1. Analyze your goals and identify the skills and expertise you must acquire in order to achieve those goals. Focus your development on those areas.

- [ ] 2. Keep a daily "to-do" list and prioritize your duties into high, medium, and low priorities.

- [ ] 3. Identify the objectives and control techniques within your area of operational responsibility.

- [ ] 4. Break challenging or large tasks into smaller, manageable tasks. When you have a project goal, develop interim goals and timelines, and force yourself to adhere to the schedule.

5. Try to keep emotions out of conflicts. Resolve the issues in terms of value added to the organization, regardless of your feelings or the people involved.

6. Develop constructive coping skills, such as managing time with well thought out strategies, reframing issues in cognitive rather than emotional terms, and breaking down problems into smaller pieces and then addressing the pieces rather than the whole.

7. Err on the conservative side if there is any question about the ethical integrity of a decision or action you are considering.

Development Plan Resources: Self-Responsibility and Management

Build your expertise by reviewing the sources listed below:

Learning and Development Resources
Centrestar Academy. *Enhancing your emotional intelligence.* www.centrestar.com
Covey, S. (2020). *The 7 habits of highly effective people: Guided journal.*
Duhigg, C. (2014). *The power of habit: Why we do what we do in life and business.*
Glei, J.K. & 99U. (2021). *Manage your day-to-day: Build your routine, find your focus, and sharpen your creative mind.*

You are in charge of your career. Remember: plan or be planned for.

Reflection and Application: Self-Responsibility and Management

Taking self-responsibility means many things, including discipline, timeliness, being proactive, reflecting on successes and failures, and communicating effectively with others. It means keeping your emotions in check and setting a good example for others.

Remember:

- Those you lead or manage will watch to see how to behave. Set a good example, even when you think that nobody is looking.

- Time-management is an important skill. Learn to be on time. Only then can you expect your people to be on time.

- Embrace diversity and treat people well. Leave any negative feelings that you may have about groups or individuals at home.

- Take time to reflect on your failures as well as your successes and learn from both.

8

The most important concept I learned about this competency is:

_____

_____

_____

_____

_____

To effectively apply this concept to my personal development I plan to:

_____

_____

_____

_____

_____

_____

_____

_____

_____

_____

Be proactive in all that you do.

COMPETENCY 9
Interpersonal Skills

IMPORTANCE (I)	DEVELOPMENT NEED (DN)	VALUE (I x DN)
1 2 3 4 5	1 2 3 4 5	

9

Appropriately sociable; interacts effectively with others.

If there is any great secret of success in life, it lies in the ability to put yourself in the other person's place and to see things from his point of view - as well as your own.

— Henry Ford[14]

Whether you are a manager, supervisor, or a leader of any title, working well with people is paramount. A leader must have technical skills and knowledge, but a leader must also know how to work with people: the ability to be sociable, to encourage, to motivate, and to lead. You must have people skills.

While some people seem to have an ability to interact well with others, do not worry if this is not you. Interpersonal skills can be learned. Developing effective interpersonal skills requires an evaluation of your current skills. You start by identifying your strengths and weaknesses, and then work to improve the areas that need attention. Finally, re-evaluate your newly developed skills and make plans for further development.

To clarify the concepts applicable to this competency read the following list of observable and measurable knowledge, skills, tasks, and behaviors essential to all professionals:

- ✓ Participates as member of a team and contributes to the group.

- ✓ Teaches others new skills.

- ✓ Serves customers/clients - works to satisfy customer expectations.

- ✓ Exercises leadership - communicates ideas to justify position, persuades and convinces others, responsibly challenges existing procedures and policies.

✓ Negotiates – works toward agreements involving exchange of resources, resolves divergent interests.

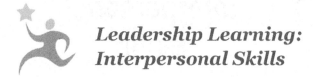

Leadership Learning:
Interpersonal Skills

The Nature of Leadership

9

Meerkats trust each other to stand guard and protect the group.

A good leader is a good coach, mentor, and role model. A leader must be able to teach others, work well with others, and, perhaps most importantly, understand and model the value of teamwork. Leaders show themselves to be team players by taking responsibility for the team, protecting them, taking the blame when things go wrong, and making the team feel safe, just like the meerkat does in the wild.

At just a couple of pounds in weight and standing a foot high, meerkats, despite having some strong teeth, are not adept at fighting predators. But what they do, and do well, is dig and run. Meerkats live in and above an intricate system of tunnels that they dig to provide shelter from the elements and protection from their enemies.

Yet, to eat and play the meerkats must be in the open, thus compromising their safety. They go above ground to forage, to enjoy the sun, and to romp in the desert. So how do they stay safe? A leader stands guard and protects them.

When meerkats venture out of their burrows, one or more meerkats take up a sentinel post. They stand at attention, on hind legs, watching the ground and the sky, on the lookout for any danger that might approach. With this little protector standing vigil the other meerkats can focus attention on other business, secure in the knowledge that the sentinel has their backs and will sound an alert if danger threatens.

An effective leader performs these same functions. Your team members should feel comfortable coming to you with questions and concerns. They should always know that you have their backs, that you are looking out for their best interests, and that you can be trusted to protect the group.

Leading by Example: Interpersonal Skills

9

Real Life Leaders

Tony Hsieh had employees start at the bottom/ground floor, so they could learn what customers needed and realize the value of good interpersonal skills.

Tony Hsieh was an amazing leader. Even if he has not become a household name, he should have. Hsieh was a self-made man, a millionaire in his twenties, one who understood the importance of interpersonal skills in business. He exemplifies these skills every day.

As former CEO of Zappos, Hsieh and his team have learned to put the customer first, by creating an amazing workforce of people who love their jobs, know their jobs, and want nothing more than to do THIS job. Under the watchful eye of Hsieh, Zappos was among the first companies in the world to begin a program of paying their employees to quit. Sounds crazy, of course. But it works.

At Zappos, employees begin at the bottom – the call center. Customer service call centers are notorious for being miserable places and no one wants to work there. However, call center employees can connect with and come to understand customers, and they can build interpersonal skills that will serve them well in whatever job they graduate to.

Hsieh and his team developed an onboarding program where new employees begin with call center training and spend a minimum amount of time working there. After their call center experience is over and they are preparing to move into a new position within the company, employees are offered up to five thousand dollars to quit Zappos, and never allowed to return. Few take up the offer. This form of "weeding out" is designed to make employees committed to and valued at Zappos, and it works. It demonstrates Hsieh's insight into teamwork, teaching others, serving customers, leadership, and negotiation.

Assess Your Skills: Interpersonal Skills

Take a moment to consider what you know about this concept and assess your skills. Indicate your level of agreement with each question.

How competent am I	Very little	Somewhat	Very much
Do I comfortably and competently interact with those above me in the chain of command?			
Do I comfortably and competently interact with those I lead?			
Am I effective at teaching and coaching others?			
Do I work well as part of a team?			
Do I satisfy customers and hold customer satisfaction in high regard?			
Am I professional in my interactions?			
Do I show respect to contractors, suppliers, and others with whom I interact?			
Do I negotiate in a way that is effective and fair for all parties?			

7 Tips – What To Do:
Interpersonal Skills

The following tips will help you become more successful and continually improve your competence in this area. Check those that you need to develop.

- ☐ 1. Consider taking an interpersonal styles inventory so that you understand and respect style differences within a group.

- ☐ 2. Demonstrate interest in your colleagues by using active listening techniques and responding positively.

- ☐ 3. Seek feedback from peers and colleagues about their perceptions of your sociability, fairness, and effectiveness with others.

- ☐ 4. Use active listening techniques when communicating with customers. Take notes on conversations.

- ☐ 5. Conduct focus groups with internal and external customers to understand what they want and expect.

- ☐ 6. Maintain a professional demeanor in interactions with every individual in the work environment.

- ☐ 7. When negotiating, do not place the other party in a position in which they may lose face. Offer choices between alternatives, which can sometimes be done by following mild demands with stronger ones, and present a cooperative attitude.

9

Development Plan Resources: Interpersonal Skills

Build your expertise by reviewing the sources listed below:

Learning and Development Resources
Centrestar Academy. *Enhancing communication in the workplace.* www.centrestar.com
Carnegie, D. (classic). *How to win friends & influence people.*
Cialdini, R.B. ((2021). *Influence: The psychology of persuasion.*
Wood, J. (2019). *The interpersonal communication: Everyday encounters.*

Consider that supervisors communicate 70 percent of the time, or more, and yet through five organizational levels, people typically understand only 20 percent. A small improvement in communication can yield big results.

Reflection and Application: Interpersonal Skills

Effective interpersonal communication involves developing the ability to listen to others and to communicate your ideas; good communication is a two-way street. Remember that listening means not just hearing but truly understanding and considering what the other person says.

Remember:

- Listen. Really listen.
- Keep your emotions in check. Do not attack people, and do not speak in anger. Take a deep breath or step away if you must.
- Be open to feedback received from others. In fact, ask for it. Learn from it.
- When negotiating, always look for the win-win, a situation in which everyone leaves the table feeling they got a good deal.
- Remember that interpersonal communications is not only about what you say, but how you listen, your body language, and your behavior.

The most important concept I learned about this competency is:

_____

_____

_____

_____

_____

_____

9

_____

_____

_____

_____

_____

_____

_____

_____

_____

_____

_____

_____

_____

_____

_____

_____

_____

_____

To effectively apply this concept to my personal development I plan to:

9

_____

_____

_____

_____

_____

_____

_____

_____

_____

_____

_____

_____

_____

_____

_____

_____

_____

_____

_____

_____

_____

_____

Take an honest interest in others and they will be interested in you.

COMPETENCY 10
Oral Communication

IMPORTANCE (I)	DEVELOPMENT NEED (DN)	VALUE (I x DN)
1 2 3 4 5	1 2 3 4 5	

Makes clear and effective oral presentations to individuals and groups; listens to others.

10

To effectively communicate, we must realize that we are all different in the way we perceive the world and use this understanding as a guide to our communication with others.

- Tony Robbins[15]

Related to interpersonal communication is the concept of oral communication. This is about being clear in what you say when giving presentations and when talking with individuals or groups. Effective communication involves not just talking, but also carefully listening. It involves asking questions to ensure that you understand the other person's point of view.

Effective oral communication also involves demeanor. When you communicate in a way that is confident, your words and ideas are more persuasive. Of course, oral communication also means presenting effectively, whether you are speaking to a team about workplace safety, presenting a proposal to a client, or giving a multimedia presentation to an entire organization.

To clarify the concepts applicable to this competency read the following list of observable and measurable knowledge, skills, tasks, and behaviors essential to all professionals:

✓ Listens to others and shows understanding of what they say.

✓ Makes clear and effective oral presentations to individuals and groups.

✓ Uses appropriate questioning techniques to gather feedback and opinions.

✓ Expresses opinions confidently, even in face of disagreement.

✓ Conveys information, opinions, and directions in concise and direct manner.

Leadership Learning:
Oral Communication

The Nature of Leadership

Western scrub jaybirds hold funerals and communicate orally.

The western scrub jay, a small blue bird native to western North America, has a unique way of communicating with others, or at least a special time when they choose to communicate. The Western scrub jay holds funerals (Walker, 2012).

If a jay spots another of its kind lying dead it will immediately stop foraging for food, move near the body, and call out a special sound. This attracts more jays who then imitate that behavior. This usually goes on for a full day, with all the birds halting whatever they are doing to rally around the deceased.

Researchers are unsure if the birds are preparing to present a united front to a potential predator, whether they are mourning in some way, or if they are just sounding an alert that something dangerous may be in the area. But the fact is that the jays, seeing only a dead body and not having witnessed an attack or manner of death, recognize that this is important information to be shared with the group and so that is what they do: They share information.

Most animals communicate orally, whether calling for a mate, announcing to others that they have found food, or shrieking to warn of or chase predators. But the jay takes oral communication to a level that seems emotional and can only be described as somewhat human.

In our human world, some individuals appear to be natural oral communicators. We illustrate the importance of oral communication by detailing and praising those who deliver great speeches. Certainly, Lincoln's Gettysburg address stands as strong testament to the longevity of the spoken word, as does Martin Luther King Jr.'s "I have a dream" speech, or the famous line by President Kennedy, "Ask not what your country can do for you, ask what you can do for your country."

The power of oral communication can never be understated, in either the animal kingdom or in our human world.

Leading by Example: Oral Communication

Real Life Leaders

10

Winston Churchill is known for his inspiring speeches during times of World War II.

Serving as Prime Minister of Britain through the 1930s and 1940s, Winston Churchill was an exceptional communicator. Churchill had a strong ability to develop extremely effective speeches (Six Leadership Traits, 2016), speeches that gave the British people faith in his leadership and a strong trust in his plans for the country.

World War II was a dark, difficult period for Europe and beyond, and certainly Britain faced its share of adversity. Churchill gave people hope using precise, easy to understand language (Six Leadership Traits, 2016). This allowed the British people to identify with his positions, and so trust that he could secure the defeat of Nazi Germany (Six Leadership Traits, 2016).

Churchill had many great leadership strengths. When it came to employing the oral communication skills in his leadership toolbox, Churchill knew that what mattered was not only what he said, but when and how he said it. Churchill is known for inspiring, uplifting speeches, including the exclamation, "What is the use of living, if it be not to strive for noble causes and to make this muddled world a better place for those who will live in it after we are gone?" (Six Leadership Traits, 2016). He instinctively knew how to motivate, encourage, and deliver hope.

Churchill also knew how to be visible to people at the right times, to use his words to lift them from despair. During the war Churchill often visited areas that were suffering, such as factories or bombed out homes (Six Leadership Traits, 2016), where he spoke words of consolation and spirit. Churchill knew that a great leader uses words not only to share information, but also uses the power of words to create emotions and bonds with his people.

Assess Your Skills: Oral Communication

Take a moment to consider what you know about this concept and assess your skills. Indicate your level of agreement with each question.

How competent am I	Very little	Somewhat	Very much
When speaking, am I clear in my enunciation, grammar, and word choice?			
When speaking, am I effective in tone, expression, and pacing?			
Am I aware of my body language and use it appropriately?			
Am I an active listener?			
Do I know how to ask questions to get the information I need and to engage positively?			
Do I know how to convey my ideas in a concise and professional way?			
Do I regularly show empathy, putting myself in the other people's shoes?			
When speaking, do I avoid excessive jargon?			

7 Tips – What To Do: Oral Communication

The following tips will help you become more successful and continually improve your competence in this area. Check those that you need to develop.

☐ 1. Try to put yourself into another person's role and anticipate how your communication is likely to be received. Interact with the speaker in nonverbal ways to show that you are listening, for example, you might nod your head, smile, and maintain eye contact.

☐ 2. Practice your listening skills by listening to the news and then testing yourself on how much you remember.

☐ 3. Practice your oral communication skills by volunteering to speak in front of groups. Opportunities in your community can be good practice. If you need to improve, take a public speaking course or join a public speaking club.

☐ 4. Ask open-ended questions that require more than a yes or no answer, and before responding to others reframe their statement or message to confirm your understanding and to provide time to formulate a response.

☐ 5. Record your conversations and then analyze them to determine how you sound to others. Consider your tone, speed, wordiness, use of "uhs," clarity, and enthusiasm.

☐ 6. Ask others to evaluate your speaking and listening skills and suggest ways to improve them. Ask them to restate what you have said to make sure that they understand. If there is no understanding, there has been no communication.

☐ 7. Prepare presentation aids that will reduce your anxiety, keep your presentation on track, and enhance the clarity of your presentation.

Development Plan Resources: Oral Communication

Build your expertise by reviewing the sources listed below:

Learning and Development Resources
Centrestar Academy. *Developing and delivering dynamic presentations.* www.centrestar.com
Duhigg, C. (2019). *Summary: The power of habit: Why we do what we do in life and business.*
Navarro, J. (2018). *The dictionary of body language: A field guide to human behavior*
Young, K.S. & Travis, H.P. (2017). *Oral communication: Skills, choices, and consequences.*

The best idea is meaningless unless it is communicated to others and they rally around it.

Reflection and Application: Oral Communication

There are many areas you can work on to improve your communications skills. Empathy can be helpful. Put yourself in the shoes of the person you are interacting with and consider their point of view. Understand how you can best express yourself to a particular person or group.

Remember:

- Show interest in others; use appropriate body language; and ask open-ended questions.
- If you do not know whether you understand what someone is saying, or if you need to buy time to formulate a response, try rephrasing the other person's statement or question before you answer.
- Practice speaking in front of groups with presentation aids such as slides or notecards, which can greatly reduce presentation anxiety.
- Believe in yourself.

The most important concept I learned about this competency is:

To effectively apply this concept to my personal development I plan to:

10

_____

_____

_____

_____

_____

_____

_____

_____

_____

_____

_____

_____

_____

_____

_____

_____

_____

_____

_____

How you speak determines your credibility.

COMPETENCY 11
Written Communication

IMPORTANCE (I)	DEVELOPMENT NEED (DN)	VALUE (I x DN)
1 2 3 4 5	1 2 3 4 5	

Communicates effectively in writing; can critically review and comprehend information written by others.

11

One of the really bad things you can do to your writing is to dress up the vocabulary, looking for long words because you're maybe a little bit ashamed of your short ones.

– Stephen King[16]

You might have heard something to the effect that in our modern world we seemingly spend less time communicating with each other, or that we talk via machines more than we do directly to people.

In reality, we communicate more with others now, in the age of technology, than ever before. In past times, people often went an entire day without going anywhere or talking to anyone outside the home. But when was the last time that you went an entire day without talking on the phone, sending an email, writing a text, or communicating in some way? It is probably rare that such a day goes by.

Today we do not often send handwritten letters or even birthday cards, but between email and texting many of us write more than ever. And in the workplace, via your computer, you are likely writing presentations, memos, and any number of reports. The ability to communicate effectively in writing is paramount in today's business world, whatever field you are in.

To clarify the concepts applicable to this competency read the following list of observable and measurable knowledge, skills, tasks, and behaviors essential to all professionals:

✓ Communicates facts and ideas in writing in a clear, succinct, and organized manner.

✓ Reviews and critiques others' writing in a constructive and substantive manner.

✓ Conveys email information, opinions, and directions in a concise and direct manner.

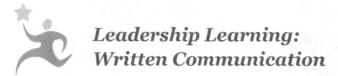

Leadership Learning: Written Communication

The Nature of Leadership

Pigeons reportedly can recognize all 26 letters of the English language.

Pigeons, gorillas, and bees understand effective communication.

One of the things that separates us from the animals is our ability as humans to effectively communicate in multiple ways. In addition to speaking and writing, we have developed numerous other methods of communication such as sign language, using facial expressions and body language, morse code, and drawing to name but a few. We have also invented a multitude of ways in which to communicate via oral, or written dissemination. We send text messages, emails, make phone and video calls, have entire conversations via social media comments, and much more. Gone are the days of smoke signals, and telegraphs but we can write, read, critically review, and comprehend books, magazines, newspapers, social media posts, blogs, and so much more. And with over 6,000 languages being utilized worldwide there is an infinite number of ways in which information can be transmitted orally, in written form, and via countless other methodologies from one person to other individuals, or massive groups.

Although those in the animal kingdom are not privy to various communication methods we use, many highly intelligent creatures who effectively communicate in their own ways. Bees and ants use pheromones to communicate, and numerous other animals communicate with specific sounds to convey certain information. Gorillas successfully communicate with humans using sign language, and pigeons recognize not only all 26 letters of the alphabet but as many as 58 four-letter words (Scarf, & Colombo, 2019).

Regardless of the method you use to disseminate information, you must be precise.

This is true with so many words and phrases holding multiple meanings. For instance, saying "I really need a date" can mean several things. Perhaps you require a particular fruit, or desire the exclusive company of another, or need to know a particular day on the calendar. As you can see, not being specific can lead to easily avoided misunderstandings. While we may no longer use carrier pigeons, we wouldn't want to confuse them (or the people with whom we are attempting to communicate) by using the wrong four-letter word.

Leading by Example: Written Communication

11

Real Life Leaders

Martin Luther King encouraged, motivated, and educated others through is writing and speeches.

Dr. Martin Luther King Jr. with his tremendous leadership skills came along at just the right time in American history. Dr. King used his abilities and the heartbeat of the country to push the rights of African Americans forward, and lift people up and give them hope. He did this in many ways, including through his innovative and peaceful protests, his commitment, and his ability to both write and speak in ways that moved people.

In his live speeches, Dr. King was motivational and uplifting. In fact, he was "one of the world's most eloquent speakers, a magisterial orator whose august style of delivery varnished even ordinary words enough to make them shine" (Broughton, n.d.). People followed his words, his ideas... his ideals. His words inspired a movement that brought change and shaped history.

Dr. King knew how to inform and educate through writing: "Darkness cannot drive out darkness; only light can do that. Hate cannot drive out hate; only love can do that." King knew how to paint a picture and take a person back in time by writing, "Five score years ago, a great American, in whose symbolic shadow we stand today, signed the Emancipation Proclamation. This momentous decree came as a great beacon light of hope to millions of Negro slaves who had been seared in the flames of withering injustice. It came as a joyous daybreak to end the long night of their captivity." Dr. King knew how to motivate and inspire, writing, "I refuse to accept the view that mankind is so tragically bound to the starless midnight of racism and war that the bright daybreak of peace and brotherhood can never become a reality... I believe that unarmed truth and unconditional love will have the final word."

As one author put it, King was "a great writer who seemed to have understood instinctively, whether he was writing a sermon, a speech, or a book, that he was writing for posterity as well as the times in which he lived." And that is what King did, writing words that not only inspired change during the civil rights movement in the United States, but that will go on into perpetuity, standing strong to inspire the ages.

Assess Your Skills: Written Communication

Take a moment to consider what you know about this concept and assess your skills. Indicate your level of agreement with each question.

How competent am I	Very little	Somewhat	Very much
Am I an effective writer?			
Do I proofread even minor writings, such as text messages?			
Do I practice good grammar in my writing?			
Do I avoid excessive use of jargon in my writing?			

Do I communicate both facts and tone in writing?			
Am I concise in my writing?			
Do I remember the audience when I write?			
Do I know how to use visual aids to make my writing more valuable to the reader?			

7 Tips - What To Do: Written Communication

The following tips will help you become more successful and continually improve your competence in this area. Check those that you need to develop.

☐ 1. Write as you speak, avoiding flowery language and unnecessary adjectives and adverbs. Action verbs are powerful when used appropriately.

☐ 2. Ask colleagues or friends to give feedback on your writing. Revise if their understanding of your ideas does not match your intent.

☐ 3. Create an outline before you start writing a report, memo, or letter. Begin your document by summarizing the main topic and any supporting concepts you will address. Use headings to alert the reader of a new idea or concept. Summarize ideas.

☐ 4. Write emails with short sentences and paragraphs, they are easier to read and understand. Remember that spelling and grammar reflect your level of professionalism.

☐ 5. Use accurate and relevant visual aids to add impact to your documents. When presenting numerical data, use charts and graphs.

☐ 6. Write for the people who will read your communication. Use language they will understand. Consider what they already know and what you want to tell them.

☐ 7. Keep technical language to a minimum when writing for a diverse group. If you use technical terminology and jargon, provide definitions and have a non-technical person review your work. For tips, draw on members of your work unit who are excellent writers.

Development Plan Resources:
Written Communication

Build your expertise by reviewing the sources listed below:

Learning and Development Resources
Centrestar Academy. *Business writing styles.* www.centrestar.com
Chaffee, J. (2014). *Critical thinking, thoughtful writing.*
Provost, G., & Grimes, P. (2019). *100 Ways to improve your writing: Proven professional techniques for writing with style and power.*
Struck, W., & White, E. (2021). *The elements of style.*

Remember the power of the pen. Those who control the meeting notes form the perceptions others will have about the meeting.

Reflection and Application:
Written Communication

Virtually all business professionals write something important in the workplace every day. They may write a memo or an email to a client, a letter to a competitor, a grant to a government agency... the list is endless.

Remember:
- Write clearly and concisely.
- Be friendly and professional. It is possible to do both at one time.
- Avoid professional jargon and short cuts like "u" when you mean "you."
- Do not write in anger. If you need to, take a break – maybe an entire day – before you craft a message and hit the Send button.
- Proofread everything you write, from simple texts to emails. A minor error can result in a misunderstanding or damage your reputation, credibility, or career.

The most important concept I learned about this competency is:

11

To effectively apply this concept to my personal development I plan to:

11

_____

_____

_____

_____

_____

_____

_____

_____

_____

_____

_____

_____

_____

_____

_____

_____

_____

_____

_____

_____

_____

The principal objective of any writing is to convey meaning to its audience.

Competency Cluster C:
Supervisory Management

If your actions create a legacy that inspires others to dream more, learn more, do more and become more, you are an excellent leader.

– Dolly Parton[17]

Being personally and professionally competent is vital to your success, and expressing that competence by leading others is essential in the team-based workplaces of today. No matter how brilliant or capable one person is, more can be accomplished when people work as a team. Although, even a talented team can accomplish little without a thoughtful, trained supervisor.

Employees trained and experienced in supervisory management are prepared to be good leaders and coaches. They know when to cheer for their team and when to direct the team. They can help prevent problems, and also help solve them, decisively, when issues arise. Conflict management is a vital part of leadership and supervision.

Helping people work together involves the ability to model and encourage **teamwork** and **cooperation**, **influence others** and **negotiate** when necessary, and **build interpersonal relationships**, yet always keep focused on the **customer**. Competency Cluster C: Supervisory Management covers ten competencies that revolve around supervisory management.

COMPETENCY 12
Leadership and Coaching

IMPORTANCE (I)	DEVELOPMENT NEED (DN)	VALUE (I x DN)
1 2 3 4 5	1 2 3 4 5	

Models and encourages high standards of ethical behavior; adapts leadership styles to situations and people; empowers, motivates, guides, and coaches.

12

If you can't describe what you are doing as a process, you don't know what you're doing.

– W. Edwards Deming[18]

This book repeatedly mentions the value of being a good role model because it is that important. There are essentially two ways you influence those you lead: through what you do and through what you say. Good leadership is a blend of being a role model and a coach through appropriate speech and actions.

Many leaders try to be cheerleaders. They are positive and happy, telling their team what a good job they are doing, patting them on the back, and giving a thumbs up. With such non-specific praise you do not influence their behavior or encourage continued good behavior in the future. In addition to being a cheerleader, be a coach. Tell people specifically what they are doing well and what they can do to improve. Guide them towards continual improvement, ethical behavior, and good decision making.

To clarify the concepts applicable to this competency, read the following list of observable and measurable knowledge, skills, tasks, and behaviors essential to all professionals:

✓ Demonstrates and encourages a high standard of honesty, integrity, trust, openness, and respect for others.

✓ Adapts leadership style to fit a variety of situations and people.

✓ Inspires, motivates, and guides others toward goal achievement.

✓ Empowers others by sharing power and authority commensurate with delegated responsibility.

✓ Coaches, mentors, and challenges others to achieve their potential.

✓ Balances mission, objectives, and resources with needs and expectations.

✓ Delegates responsibility and authority.

✓ Maintains visibility, credibility, and consistency.

✓ Creates and promotes an open, healthy environment in which others feel valued.

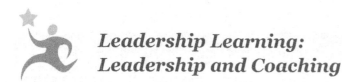

Leadership Learning:
Leadership and Coaching

The Nature of Leadership

12

Mountain Goats lead and rally behind frightened goats.

Everyone needs encouragement at one point or another, even mountain goats who spend a lot of time on the move, living a nomadic life. They hop, with surprising ease, from precipice to precipice, alluding predators, finding food, and staying with their herd.

Goats must often traverse rough boulder-strewn mountain streams filled with rapidly moving white water. This can be intimidating, especially for smaller goats. When they must cross such a stream, the goats go one by one but do so by working together. The leading goat hops from stone to stone, crossing the water quickly. The other goats watch and then follow. When a smaller or timid goat's turn comes, the goat may balk at braving the rapids by standing on the river's edge and bleating loudly.

Do the other goats just move on, ignoring the frantic call? No. They rally behind the frightened goat. Often, one goat – perhaps a parent or simply a leader – hops partway back across the raging water until it is near the timid goat. The leader then calls to the goat, encouraging it to take a leap of faith and jump to the next rock. The timid goat bleats with worry. The leader calls again. Eventually, the leader persuades the timid goat to leap from the safety of the rock and make its way across the rapids. The herd moves on, with all members present.

Leadership and coaching are a phenomenon repeatedly seen throughout nature. As humans, we lead our families and coach our children, but we can also do this with colleagues and those we supervise. Sometimes we lead because we have a title. Other times we lead because people sense something in us and feel the urge to follow. Either way, every supervisor and leader must set a good example and encourage others in the group, team, or organization.

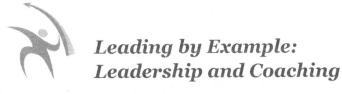

Leading by Example: Leadership and Coaching

Real Life Leaders

Mike Krzyzewski and Cael Sanderson show how sports serve as a metaphor for the challenges and joys of life.

Undoubtedly, we will all face challenges in life where we must deal with situations that have us wrestling with our consciouses, struggling to take the high-road, and living up to the standards of ethical behavior we (as well as others) have set for ourselves. No matter how adept we may become at facilitating a principled lifestyle, challenges are inevitable. Even the most morally upright leaders and coaches among us will struggle from time to time. But one foundation of solid leadership is the capacity for rising above these situations to empower, motivate, and guide those around us to the best of our abilities.

Perhaps two of the best contemporary coaches in college athletics today are legendary Coach K, Mike Krzyzewski, former head coach of men's basketball at Duke University and Cael Sanderson, head wrestling coach at Penn State. There are many similarities between the two coaches. One is that recruiting for their cultures is a tight-knit family affair. Another is that both encourage academic excellence as well as developing personal relationships in which they can trust talking about their personal lives and aspirations. And finally, their simplistic and consistent approach to coaching is you cannot ask anything of those you are leading that you are not willing to do as well.

Coach Mike Krzyzewski in addition to being the winningest college basketball coach, is also a world-class speaker and author who personifies coaching and leadership success. Enter his name into a search engine, and you will find a long list of things to read. Or look online for books and again you will see many choices.

We also suggest that you look at his website, http://coachk.com. Of special notice to those of us interested in leadership are many of Coach K's well-known quotes.

Here are a just a few. Think about how his ideas apply to your situation, and how you can use the ideas to make yourself a better leader.

Are You Committed to Being a Leader?

Here is an excellent place to start. Coach K says: "I don't look at myself as a basketball coach. I look at myself as a leader who happens to coach basketball."

No matter your background or profession, do you first think of yourself as a leader?

Are You Doing What You Want to Do?

How did you decide to accept your current job? Is it what you want to do? Coach K says:

> "I've never made a decision based on what will get me the most money. It was what was going to give me the most happiness and I've been really happy and fulfilled at Duke."

If you do not enjoy your work, everyone will know it. Your ability to build a successful career starts with the decision you make about what you want to do, and the decisions you make along the way.

Communication

Communication is not so much a problem when everything is great. However, there will be times when things are not so great.

Do you do speak the truth, even when that truth is uncomfortable? Do you encourage your team to do the same? All the time?

Here is what Coach K says:

> "Confrontation simply means meeting the truth head on."

> "In our program, the truth is the basis of all that we do. There is nothing more important than the truth because there is nothing more powerful than the truth. Consequently, on our team, we always tell one another the truth. We must be honest with one another. There is no other way."

Faith in Yourself and Others

You cannot lead if you do not believe you can succeed. Coach K reminds us of this when he says:

> "Believe that the loose ball that you are chasing has your name on it."

> "Confidence shared is better than confidence only in yourself."

Do you believe in yourself? If not, why not? Do you have faith in others?

Teams

Here are some of Coach K's ideas about teams. They apply to all teams everywhere:

> "People want to be on a team. They want to be part of something bigger than themselves. They want to be in a situation where they feel that they are doing something for the greater good."

> "People have to be given the freedom to show the heart they possess. I think it's a leader's responsibility to provide that type of freedom. And I believe it can be done through relationships and family. Because if a team is a real family, it's members want to show you their hearts."

Trust

Finally, if you are to lead, remember that while you may have a title, you also must earn the right. Coach K says:

> "Every leader needs to remember that a healthy respect for authority takes time to develop. It's like building trust. You don't instantly have trust, it has to be earned."

As for Cael Sanderson, he is a model of coaching and leadership.

Someone who has literally wrestled with difficulties and emerged victorious time and time again is legendary college wrestler, Olympic gold medalist, and Penn State wrestling coach, Cael Sanderson. With an unbelievable college record of

12

159-0 (NCAA.com, 2020), Sanderson truly exemplifies the high standards that are imperative to successful leadership and proves that sports serve as a metaphor for the challenges and joys of life.

Making the move from wrestler to coach, Sanderson has continued his streak of excellence, leading Penn State to multiple national NCAA championships and instilling within his wrestlers not only the attributes and traits needed to become successful athletes, but also leaders in their own rights. Cael Sanderson personifies the most important traits a coach (or leader) can exhibit and encourages his underlings to do the same. He models and encourages high standards of ethical behavior; adapts his leadership styles to situations and people; empowers, motivates, guides, and coaches those within his circle of influence. Although some of us may never be record-setting athletes, we can all strive to personify Sanderson's commitment to excellence in all aspects of our lives.

12

Assess Your Skills: Leadership and Coaching

Take a moment to consider what you know about this concept and assess your skills. Indicate your level of agreement with each question.

How competent am I	Very little	Somewhat	Very much
Am I an effective and positive role model?			
Do I know the difference between cheerleading and coaching in the workplace?			
Do I empower others to do their best?			
Am I an effective motivator and guide?			
Do I know how to balance the needs of the organization with the needs of individual team members?			
Do others view me as a leader?			
Do I work to promote an open and healthy environment?			
In interactions, am I respectful of feelings and privacy?			

7 Tips - What To Do:
Leadership and Coaching

The following tips will help you become more successful and continually improve your competence in this area. Check those that you need to develop.

☐ 1. Serve as a role model of integrity in your work and lead by example. Instill your values in everything you do.

☐ 2. Always maintain a professional demeanor in interactions with everyone in the workplace and leave time in your day for informal discussions related to work.

☐ 3. Show support and respect to others when they seek your advice about their work. If you have anything negative to say, do it in private and do not share the information with others.

☐ 4. Seek role models at all levels of your organization who display leadership and learn from them.

☐ 5. Consult with people you respect if you experience difficulty managing employee performance.

☐ 6. Clearly define the decisions individuals are authorized to make and those that require approval.

☐ 7. Enhance your coaching skills by attending a workshop or course, or read a book, and practice what you learn.

12

Development Plan Resources: Leadership and Coaching

Build your expertise by reviewing the following sources listed:

Learning and Development Resources
Centrestar Academy. *Developing performance coaching techniques.* www.centrestar.com
Stanier, M. (2016). *The coaching habit: Say less, ask more & change the way you lead forever*
Kosterlitz, A. (2019). *Fearless feedback: A guide for coaching leaders to see themselves more clearly and galvanize growth.*
Krzyzewski, M. (2001). *Leading with the heart: Coach K's successful strategies for basketball, business, and life.*

Training can increase productivity by over 20 percent. Training plus coaching can result in nearly a 90 percent increase!

Reflection and Application: Leadership and Coaching

An effective leader is one who empowers, motivates, guides, and coaches, and is not just a cheerleader. Effective leaders surround themselves with people they trust, then delegate responsibility and authority to those people, giving them the opportunity to develop and excel. An effective leader inspires and motivates.

Remember:

- Sometimes you need to adapt your leadership style to fit people and situations. Some people might respond to firm leadership, while others need a moderate hand.

- A good leader shares the glory with the team but takes responsibility for problems that may arise. This builds trust and loyalty from team members.

The most important concept I learned about this competency is:

_____

_____

_____

_____

_____

_____

_____

12

_____

_____

_____

_____

_____

_____

_____

_____

_____

_____

_____

_____

_____

_____

_____

To effectively apply this concept to my personal development I plan to:

12

_____

_____

_____

_____

_____

_____

_____

_____

_____

_____

_____

_____

_____

_____

_____

_____

_____

_____

_____

_____

_____

A good leader wears many hats.

COMPETENCY 13
Flexibility and Resilience

IMPORTANCE (I)	DEVELOPMENT NEED (DN)	VALUE (I x DN)
1 2 3 4 5	1 2 3 4 5	

Adapts to change in the work environment; effectively copes with stress and ambiguity.

Do not repeat the tactics which have gained you one victory, but let your methods be regulated by the infinite variety of circumstances.

- Sun Tzu c. 490 BC, Chinese military strategist[19]

13

A psychologist said, "If you stand in your strength too long then it becomes your weakness" (Porter, as cited in Staub, 2008). Change is inevitable. Times change, society changes, technology changes, values change, and therefore leaders must adapt to change. Leaders must be resilient and flexible, anticipate unexpected events, and prepare to deal with eventualities.

Life is not always clear, nor are the solutions to complicated situations always readily visible. Flexibility allows a leader to look for various ways to solve problems and handle situations. Leader who can modify their response to fit circumstances are far more likely to experience success.

To clarify the concepts applicable to this competency, read the following list of observable and measurable knowledge, skills, tasks, and behaviors essential to all professionals:

✓ Adapts behavior and work methods in response to ambiguity, new information, changing conditions, or unexpected obstacles.

✓ Listens to and considers others' views, values, and needs; is open-minded.

✓ Changes or modifies decisions, policies, or direction based on new information or expectations.

✓ Functions effectively in an environment of ambiguity, uncertainty, and change.

✓ Copes effectively with job pressures and stress.

Leadership Learning: Flexibility and Resilience

The Nature of Leadership

Camels are resilient animals built for survival.

Successful leaders employ many significant characteristics and traits. Two of the most important ones for leaders in any capacity are flexibility and resilience. This may come as a surprise, but few animals exhibit these same attributes more than camels. Camels are built for survival; they can go for months on end with neither food nor water. They can lose up to 25 percent of their body weight in water and up to 30 percent during times of extreme dehydration (Ali et al., 2019).

The significant stress these extreme fluctuations cause is virtually unparalleled and there is much to be said for the adaptability and coping mechanisms camels exhibit during such periods. While humans can typically survive for several weeks without food, it only takes three to four days to succumb to dehydration. Although it may be difficult to imaging a scenario in which a leader would be forced to undergo such strenuous working conditions that they were deprived of food or water, many individuals can identify with experiencing stress so severe that it causes physical discomfort.

Managing stress is another essential tool in the leadership arsenal. While camels are typically followers, we can learn from them about stress. Camels not only survive but they thrive during extreme fluctuations in food and water. They store excess fat in their humps, which they then convert to energy and water when needed.

Humans can take a cue from these actions and store up a reserve of stress fighting tactics to help deal with life's more nerve-racking situations. One way to do this is by practicing the art of mindfulness, and other stress-coping methodologies, in times of calm. Then you can more easily recall and implement these techniques when situations become hectic.

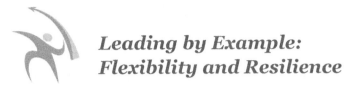

Leading by Example: Flexibility and Resilience

Real Life Leaders

Mahatma Gandhi famously said, "Be the change you want to see in the world."

One of the better known quotes ever printed on a coffee mug comes from Indian civil rights leader Mahatma Gandhi. The beautiful and elegant quote shows the flexibility and resilience of Gandhi's character: "Be the change you want to see in the world."

Gandhi lived the ideal of peaceful change. He showed resilience time and again by turning away from hatred and repression and pursuing innovative ideologies (Alain, 2012).

As we have said repeatedly, no one leader exemplifies all 35 of our leadership traits perfectly, just as no one leader can be pigeon-holed to a single trait. Gandhi's most evident leadership characteristics were "resilience, knowledge, people-skills, motivational approach and leading by example" (Alain, 2012).

Gandhi was modern India's great spiritual and political leader, helping his people rebel against the British Empire and its repression. But his tools in the fight for change were peaceful: non-cooperation and demonstration. During his time, Gandhi embodied many great leadership qualities, including a belief in growth and change (Mahatma Gandhi, 2016), the power of the word "No" to deny wrongful treatment, and that his vision was the right one (Mahatma Gandhi, 2016). Gandhi was a great

13

leader, and his vision and words continue to live and inspire 75 years after his death and will likely continue for years to come.

Assess Your Skills:
Flexibility and Resilience

Take a moment to consider what you know about this concept and assess your skills. Indicate your level of agreement with each question.

How competent am I	Very little	Somewhat	Very much
Am I flexible?			
Do I cope well with change?			
Am I open to the views and opinions of others, both my manager and my employees?			
Do I champion change in the workplace?			
In the past year have I adapted well to change?			
Do I effectively manage stress?			

7 Tips - What To Do:
Flexibility and Resilience

The following tips will help you become more successful and continually improve your competence in this area. Check those that you need to develop.

☐ 1. Analyze how you have adapted to changes in the past year. Are you flexible and willing to change? Know yourself and your reactions to crises. Plan extra time up front if you are uncomfortable with last-minute changes.

☐ 2. When making a decision, consider the down-side if the expected does not happen and prepare by making alternative plans.

☐ 3. To the extent possible develop a disciplined decision-making structure within your work group so that efficient decision-making becomes routine.

☐ 4. Enjoy the diversity of dispositions and capabilities in your work unit. Capitalize on the diversity by devising ways to draw individuals with unique talents into the work process.

13

☐ 5. List the situations that currently give you the most stress.

☐ 6. Learn and use stress reduction techniques such as deep breathing, mental imagery, deep relaxation, and meditation. Engage in physical exercise on a regular basis; eat sensibly and get enough sleep.

☐ 7. Recognize that not all stress is bad. It can give you the edge to accomplish a challenging task. Try to look at stress from a positive viewpoint and develop constructive coping skills, such as time-management strategies, reframing issues in cognitive rather than in emotional terms, breaking problems into smaller pieces, and then addressing the pieces rather than the whole.

Development Plan Resources: Flexibility and Resilience

Build your expertise by reviewing the sources listed below:

Learning and Development Resources
Centrestar Academy. *Understanding supervisory roles and functions.* www.centrestar.com
Covey, S.R. (2020). *The 7 habits of highly effective people (30th anniversary edition).*
Fullan, M. (2020). *Leading in a culture of change.*
Telford, O. (2019). *Mindfulness: The remarkable truth behind meditation and being present in your life.*

Approximately a quarter of all employees are fully engaged in their work; a quarter are fully disengaged, and the rest are in the middle. Leaders must be flexible and help people in the middle become engaged.

Reflection and Application: Flexibility and Resilience

Resilience and flexibility are essential leadership skills. Some people seem to embrace change more easily than others. But anyone can learn to be flexible and handle change in a positive way. Remember, when you embrace new circumstances, you are modeling this positive attribute for your employees.

Remember:

- Flexibility is essential in every leader, in every field.
- While some people are born resilient, anyone can learn how to adapt to change in a positive way.
- Flexibility is one aspect of emotional intelligence.
- View change as an opportunity. Sometimes it is inevitable, and embracing the change will yield more positive outcomes than resisting it.

The most important concept I learned about this competency is:

_____

_____

_____

To effectively apply this concept to my personal development I plan to:

_____

_____

_____

_____

_____

_____

_____

The best laid plans often go awry, so you must be flexible and resilient.

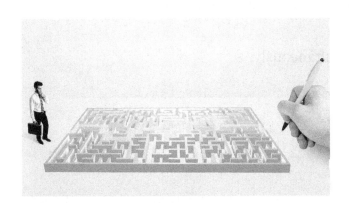

COMPETENCY 14
Problem Solving

IMPORTANCE (I)	DEVELOPMENT NEED (DN)	VALUE (I x DN)
1 2 3 4 5	1 2 3 4 5	

Recognizes and defines problems; analyzes relevant information; encourages alternative solutions, develops plans to solve problems.

Man is unique in that he has plans, purpose and goals which require the need for criteria of choice. The need for ethical value is within man whose future may largely be determined by the choice he makes.

— George Bernard Shaw[20]

14

We encounter problems constantly throughout our lives and the need to solve problems starts early. We must figure out how to crawl, walk, communicate, or even decide whether to pet the neighbor's dog. The problems we face grow in complexity as we mature, but it helps to recognize that problem solving is not a single skill. Instead, it is a way of thinking. A person who has developed good problem-solving skills knows how to apply critical thinking and planning to shape their environment and make things happen (Watanabe, 2009).

All problems involve two things: goals and barriers ("Problem Solving," n.d.). In short, something gets in the way of what you want. Solving the problem is building a bridge across the barrier to reach your goal.

To clarify the concepts applicable to this competency, read the following list of observable and measurable knowledge, skills, tasks, and behaviors essential to all professionals:

- ✓ Anticipates potential problems, issues, and opportunities.

- ✓ Encourages employees and others to identify potential problems and obstacles and initiate problem-solving processes.

- ✓ Recognizes and defines a problem or issue, gathers the data, and distinguishes between relevant and irrelevant information.

- ✓ Uses qualitative and quantitative data and analytical tools to solve problems.

✓ Encourages the development of alternative solutions and plans to solve problems.

✓ Addresses different problem simultaneously.

Leadership Learning: Problem Solving

The Nature of Leadership

The owner of a pet rat provides the rat with a small cardboard box in which he has placed a treat. The end flaps overlap so the box is tightly closed. The pet owner sits and waits to see how, or if, the rat will solve the problem of opening the box in order to retrieve the treat. The owner postulates that the rat might try to squeeze through the flaps, or even pull them open with its teeth. But within minutes the rat simply chews through the box using the tool most readily available (teeth) to get what it wants.

14

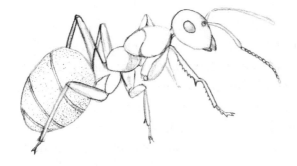

Ants obtain input from others and make collective decisions on facts.

Many animals are capable of highly sophisticated problem solving through the use of their innate abilities. Consider ants, those pesky picnic pilferers that are abundant in cartoons and kitchens around the world. When faced with a manmade obstacle course between their nest and a food source, ant scouts quickly find the shortest possible route to the food, and then other ants follow to help carry the food back home.

One study shows that ants are capable of adapting when things get tough (UOS, 2010). When the route the ants previously found is suddenly blocked, they quickly locate an alternative route, often going around, under, or over the obstacle. Once a temporary route is established and food is back in the supply line, the scout ants will return to the problem of finding the most direct and desirable path to the food. In short, scout ants solve the immediate problem with a temporary solution before they work on re-establishing the optimal solution.

As a leader you can probably solve many difficulties by acting just like the rat and chew straight through the problem to get to the answer. Yet, it will be more effective in the long run to think about the solution, obtain input from others, including your employees, and make decisions based on facts. Yes, sometimes immediate action is needed to stop something from getting worse or to simply get things done, like the ants finding a temporary path to food. Once in place, however, do not let a temporary solution become permanent. Like the scout ants, go back to looking for the optimal solution.

Leading by Example: Problem Solving

Real Life Leaders

Ken Chenault maintained a steady focus on where to go in good times and bad.

Retired American Express CEO Ken Chenault revealed that he always tried to take on challenging assignments that no one else wanted – particularly early in his career – so that he could learn (Yakowicz, 2013). That desire to learn, push, and grow is key for any leader. Such an attitude can be particularly effective in becoming an exceptional problem solver.

Chenault believes that knowing how to lead a company through both the smooth and the rough is about connecting with employees, gaining their loyalty, and being decisive (Yakowicz, 2013). As CEO of American Express since 2001, Chenault saw the company through both good times and bad. His strong, stable leadership is admired by many.

14

When other companies were feeling the pain of the 2008 recession, the disastrous times affecting the credit community, Chenault held fast to the principles and vision of AMX. Being steadfast in the face of pressure was one of Chenault's essential skills, but his ability to hope in the face of adversity is what set Chenault apart. For Chenault, a problem needs to be analyzed and solved – but the solution always starts with having a vision of where he wants to be when he gets to the other side, as well as owning the belief that he will arrive.

Assess Your Skills: Problem Solving

Take a moment to consider what you know about this concept and assess your skills. Indicate your level of agreement with each question.

How competent am I	Very little	Somewhat	Very much
Do I have a procedure for solving problems that arise in my work?			
Do I understand how to set goals and work towards achieving them?			
Am I adept at recognizing the barriers between me and my goals?			
Do I encourage my employees to solve problems on their own?			
Do I understand how to use qualitative tools in problem solving?			
Do I know how to use quantitative tools in problem solving?			
Am I a good problem solver?			

14

7 Tips - What To Do: Problem Solving

The following tips will help you become more successful and continually improve your competency in this area. Check those that you need to develop.

☐ 1. Ensure that all involved agree on the definition of the problem.

2. Before you begin to solve a problem, identify the data that you need in order to reach a solution and how that data can best be obtained. Consider adopting a round-robin discussion so that the people involved have an opportunity to express their views.

3. Have the group identify their most important concerns and suggest ways the concerns can be overcome.

4. Solicit input in order to understand differing perceptions of the problem.

5. With a behavioral problem, such as low morale or absenteeism, look to understand what the underlying problem or the root cause is. Do not treat only the symptoms.

6. Develop strategies to consider multiple-decision alternatives, including a worst-case scenario for each decision.

7. Develop disciplined decision processes in your work group whereby all elements of the decision must be supported with researched information. Avoid groupthink. Require members of your work unit to research and argue alternative viewpoints.

14

Development Plan Resources: Problem Solving

Build your expertise by reviewing the sources listed below:

Learning and Development Resources

Centrestar Academy. *Solving problems and making ethical decisions.* www.centrestar.com

Conn, C. (2019). *Bulletproof problem solving: The one skill that changes everything.*

Schwarzman, S. (2019). *What it takes: Lessons in the pursuit of excellence.*

Thinknetic (2021). *Critical thinking in a nutshell: How to become an independent thinker and make intelligent decisions.*

The cost of dysfunctional teams is high and may consume over 25 percent of a manager's time.

Reflection and Application: Problem Solving

Many problems start or continue because people do not recognize there is a problem ("Problem Solving", n.d.). You must always evaluate your relationships and situations so that you recognize potential problems before they manifest, and so you can uncover existing problems before they become crises.

Remember:

- Many problem-solving models are available to you. Generally, the models include steps such as: identifying that a problem exists, defining the problem and ensuring that everyone agrees, putting the problem into perspective, considering possible solutions to the problem, choosing and implementing one of the solutions, then evaluating the success of the solution. You may complete these steps and solve the problem in an instant, or it can take days, weeks, months, or even years.

- Sometimes, if the solution is not effective, you need to start over and repeat the process.

The most important concept I learned about this competency is:

_____

_____

_____

To effectively apply this concept to my personal development I plan to:

_____

_____

_____

_____

Problem solving is a process, but once the decision is made,
commit to it, and stay strong.

14

COMPETENCY 15
Decisiveness

IMPORTANCE (I)	DEVELOPMENT NEED (DN)	VALUE (I x DN)
1 2 3 4 5	1 2 3 4 5	

Decides and responds; makes difficult decisions as necessary.

Power is the faculty or capacity to act, the strength and potency to accomplish something. It is the vital energy to make choices and decisions. It also includes the capacity to overcome deeply embedded habits and to cultivate higher, more effective ones.

– Stephen R. Covey[21]

15

We said that problem solving sometimes happens in an instant while at other times it can take days, weeks, months, or years. You may think of decisiveness as implying speed – that you must make a decision quickly. But while timely action is one facet of being decisive, it really is more about making a final decision, perhaps a difficult decision, and then doing what it takes to see that the decision is carried through to its conclusion.

Being decisive often involves taking a risk. Decisive leaders are not always right, but they are proactive; they stay cool when the pressure is on, take charge of the situation, and display purpose and direction.

Being decisive requires a mental commitment, by which you actively decide that you will be decisive ("How to be," n.d.). If you are not a decisive leader now, you will need to develop this challenging leadership trait ("How to be", n.d.).

To clarify the concepts applicable to this competency, read the following list of observable and measurable knowledge, skills, tasks, and behaviors essential to all professionals:

- ✓ Acts decisively on own authority when timely action is required, even in uncertain situations.

- ✓ Makes difficult or unpopular decisions when necessary.

✓ Takes calculated risks to move initiatives forward.

✓ Practices participative or consensus decision-making when appropriate.

✓ Empowers employees to take appropriate risks; allows employees to fail.

Leadership Learning: Decisiveness

The Nature of Leadership

Bees act decisively to pursue rewarding endeavors or fly away.

The often heard phrase "make a bee line" to somewhere means to head quickly towards a particular locale. This expression comes from the fact that bees are extremely decisive. They respond quickly when their presence is required, such as when it is necessary to protect the queen, flee from danger, or pollinate. A lesser known bit of bee lore is that they are social animals and although they are quick to make decisions, many of the decision-making processes are a group effort.

Such is the case when a colony is seeking a new nesting area. A number of scout bees will locate several possible options and communicate the locales via dance to their assigned swarms. Swarms consist of approximately 5 percent of the bees in their hive.

The length and number of times the dance is repeated indicates the perceived quality of the potential nesting location. Once an appropriate site has been chosen by the swarm, they will alert the other members of their hive by piping (producing a specific auditory signal) (Beekman, & Oldroyd, 2018).

This process is not unlike those in many human interactions. For instance, when someone is house-hunting they typically meet with a real estate agent who then finds several suitable options for the buyer to explore. This process continues until the buyer chooses a home and makes an offer. During economic times when the housing market is considered a "seller's market," potential homebuyers must decide and act quickly to procure their desired residence. Often, many others are in the market for a home and are scouting the same locations, and thus the dance continues until they each find an acceptable domicile.

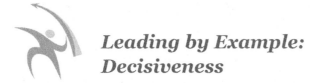

Leading by Example: Decisiveness

Real Life Leaders

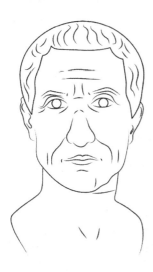

Julies Caesar believed in creating friends, taking risks, making difficult decisions.

Julius Caesar was a great politician and soldier, a leader and a warrior. Famous for the quote, "I came, I saw, I conquered," it was Caesar's communication skills, charisma, determination, and decisiveness that made him so effective in expanding the power of Rome and that set him apart in history.

From an early age, Caesar understood that making friends allowed him to influence people, that making people feel good gave him power, and that standing out from a crowd gave him notoriety. He took clear, decisive action to achieve these things, to make himself a person who was admired and feared.

As an enlisted military man of just 25, Caesar was captured by pirates and held for ransom, so the story goes. Caesar was so creative, decisive, and cunning that he soon had the pirates eating out of his hand. Caesar convinced the pirates to up his ransom and send one of his men to collect it. It took the man over a month, during which time Caesar acted as though he were the leader of the pirates, forcing his will on

15

them, but also entertaining them and inspiring their affection for him. In fact, they came to respect him, even though Caesar threatened the pirates he would have them

all killed after the ransom was paid. They brushed this off as arrogance, feeling they had all become friends. Eventually the ransom was paid, and Caesar was freed, but he returned to the island where he was held captive, stole back the ransom and the pirates' treasure, and saw to it they were all killed.

As a politician and leader, Caesar took decisive action to reform Rome's constitution, limit government terms, and implement multiple economic and social improvements. In the end, many believe that it was his quest for power – his desire to be more of a king than a ruler of a republic – that led to his undoing. But that does not diminish the fact that his ability to wield his authority, to take risks, and to make difficult decisions served Rome well.

Assess Your Skills: Decisiveness

15

Take a moment to consider what you know about this concept and assess your skills. Indicate your level of agreement with each question.

How competent am I	Very little	Somewhat	Very much
Am I decisive?			
Do I have confidence in my decisions?			
Do I empower others to be decisive and make decisions?			
Can I make difficult even unpopular decisions when necessary?			
Am I willing to take a risk to move something forward?			
Do I ask for, and give due consideration to, the opinions of others?			

7 Tips – What To Do: Decisiveness

The following tips will help you become more successful and continually improve your competency in this area. Check those that you need to develop.

☐ 1. Avoid jumping to conclusions by defining the problem in terms of solutions, as this may result in overlooking alternative, possibly better, outcomes.

☐ 2. Rather than you ask someone for an opinion about a decision, choose one alternative and develop a rationale for why that alternative is best. Then ask for input.

☐ 3. Set a target deadline by which you will arrive at a decision. For a complex decision, create a flowchart with several decision points. If many individuals or groups are involved, or if data needs to be collected, establish a timeline that shows what actions must be taken to meet the target date.

☐ 4. Involve those who will be most affected by a controversial decision to be part of the problem-solving process.

☐ 5. Use a factual approach to decision making by systematically collecting valid and reliable data. Rely on data rather than on emotion, even if the decision is unpopular. Also, explain decisions in terms of data, not emotion.

☐ 6. Avoid the need to gather and analyze an excessive amount of data before a decision can be made.

☐ 7. Before making a decision, and especially when the decision must be made under the pressure of time, consult with respected experts.

Development Plan Resources: Decisiveness

Build your expertise by reviewing the sources listed below:

Learning and Development Resources

Centrestar Academy. *Applying systematic problem solving.*
www.centrestar.com

Heath, C. & Heath, D. (2020). *Decisive: How to make better choices in life and work.*

Kahneman, D. (2013). *Thinking, fast and slow.*

Martin, C. (2014). *Moral decision making: How to approach everyday ethics.*

The meat and potatoes of supervision is making decisions and handling problems. If there were no problems, organizations would not need supervisors.

Reflection and Application: Decisiveness

The opening sequence of Star Trek the Next Generation included the phrase, "To boldly go where no one has gone before." Why boldly go? Why not just go? Well, boldly sounds more interesting. It rings better in the ear. But there is also meaning in the phrase. In that movie people were fearless. They had to be bold – and decisive – to move forward into great unknowns. Just as great leaders like you need to do.

Remember:

- To be decisive you must act confidently and with authority.
- Sometimes being decisive is just as much about *appearing* decisive.
- Thinking that you are indecisive is counter-productive. Be positive and tell yourself that you *are* decisive. Strive to be decisive and you will be.
- Sometimes decisive people make bad decisions; however, they learn from it and move on.
- Long term indecisiveness is a decision in itself, a decision to let something or someone besides you decide what will happen ("How to be", n.d.).

The most important concept I learned about this competency is:

_____

_____

_____

_____

To effectively apply this concept to my personal development I plan to:

_____

_____

_____

_____

_____

Confidence is paramount to leadership.

15

COMPETENCY 16
Self-Direction

IMPORTANCE (I)	DEVELOPMENT NEED (DN)	VALUE (I x DN)
1 2 3 4 5	1 2 3 4 5	

Realistically assesses own strengths and weaknesses; invests in self-development; demonstrates self-confidence; works persistently toward a goal; manages time effectively.

Be thou the rainbow in the storms of life. The evening beam that smiles the clouds away, and tints tomorrow with prophetic ray.

— Lord Byron[22]

By reading this book, taking notes, engaging with the content, and creating a development plan for yourself, you are showing self-direction. Great start! But keep reading this competency anyway. Effective leaders are proactive in developing their skills and working to improve themselves. The Japanese have a saying in business, Kaizen. It means focus on continual improvement.

Improvement is not simply about finding ways to make better products or improve organizational processes. It is also about improving yourself. In today's world you do not graduate from high school or college knowing all you need to know. The world changes quickly, and your knowledge needs to grow with it. You must proactively expand your knowledge and skills all the time.

To clarify the concepts applicable to this competency, read the following list of observable and measurable knowledge, skills, tasks, and behaviors essential to all professionals:

✓ Realistically assesses own strengths, weaknesses, and impact on others.

✓ Seeks and makes use of feedback from others. Able to accept criticism.

✓ Works persistently toward an agreed-upon goal despite opposition, distractions, and setbacks. Is self-disciplined.

✓ Demonstrates confidence and faith in own ability and ideas.

✓ Invests time and energy in self-development and growth, especially through training and education.

✓ Manages time effectively and efficiently.

✓ Initiates appropriate action without being directed to do so.

✓ Takes responsibility for self and actions.

✓ Works toward goals and results.

✓ Maintains high personal and professional standards.

✓ Maintains balance of personal and professional needs and demands.

Leadership Learning: Self-Direction

The Nature of Leadership

16

Polar bears are realistic and precise. They know the exact moment to catch their prey.

It has been said that "timing is everything." Anyone who has decided to take up running for the first time during the middle of the summer in the southern USA can attest to this fact. While the goal most likely is to improve health and further self-development, there are better ways to go about achieving this result.

When creating goals, it is important to realistically assess your strengths and weaknesses. If an individual hasn't run since playing a rousing game of tag during recess in elementary school, it is probably not a good idea to jump into a summer running regimen in June in a sub-tropical climate in the hopes of completing a half marathon in August. Instead, you would be better to pick a time to begin training that is less likely to result in heat stroke, to work persistently toward a more realistic goal, such as completing a 5k in November.

While it is important to invest in oneself, it is also imperative that this be done in a manner that will produce the best results. Knowing when and how to not only set but pursue goals is essential.

Creating unrealistic expectations can have detrimental effects on your morale and self-confidence. Take for instance polar bears. Their main goal is to find sustenance to ensure their survival. Although they are not particularly adept at retrieving the eggs of seabirds (Jagielski et al., 2021), they excel at catching seals and know precisely when and how to snag their prey.

Polar bears can be extremely patient, standing by a river of spawning salmon for quite some time, waiting for just the right moment to attack to ensure they are effective in their hunts. Polar bears seem to understand that timing may not be everything, but it is an essential component for success.

Leading by Example: Self-Direction

16

Real Life Leaders

Angelina Jolie had to make a difficult health decision.

When one thinks of the great leaders of our time, A-lister Hollywood actors rarely make the cut; however, world-renowned actress Angelina Jolie is one exception. She exemplifies the leadership trait of self-direction.

As an actor, Jolie has played many roles, from troubled youth to spy, archeologist to assassin. In her private life, she is a humanitarian, activist, and supporter of many causes, including improving the lives of children in disadvantaged countries. However, one decision unequivocally demonstrates her incredible self-direction and fearlessness above all others– her pre-emptive double mastectomy.

Jolie was 37 years old when doctors told her she carries the BRCA1 gene, a gene that gives her a high chance of developing breast or ovarian cancer. Having lost her mother to cancer, Jolie faced a painful decision. She had to decide whether to take her chances or reduce her chance of developing breast cancer by opting for a double mastectomy. That is an excruciating decision for anyone to make, and certainly painful for a woman known for her physical beauty. Jolie decided the surgery was worth the peace of mind.

Jolie's demonstration of self-direction – her ability to make a difficult decision about her life – did not stop there. She went public with her decision and so helped empower other women to make informed decisions about their health, and to keep themselves and families in mind without fear that such a surgery would change who they were as women, mothers, or people. Her decision to care for her health and to advocate for others demonstrates strength of mind, self-confidence, and self-direction, all of which are traits of a leader.

16

Assess Your Skills: Self-Direction

Take a moment to consider what you know about this concept and assess your skills. Indicate your level of agreement with each question.

How competent am I	Very little	Somewhat	Very much
Do I understand my most valuable strengths?			
Am I proactive in my thinking and actions?			
Do I recognize my weaknesses?			
Am I working every day to improve myself and eliminate weaknesses?			
Do I have confidence in my abilities?			
Do my managers have confidence in me?			

Do my team members and employees have confidence in me?			
Am I goal oriented?			

7 Tips – What To Do: Self-Direction

The following tips will help you become more successful and continually improve your competence in this area. Check those that you need to develop.

- ☐ 1. Analyze your career goals and the skills and expertise you lack to achieve those goals. Focus development in those areas.

- ☐ 2. Consult with a trusted mentor who has the career experiences and skills that are valued in your organization. Exploit development opportunities in temporary assignments or task forces.

- ☐ 3. If feasible, force yourself to finish a project before moving on to another by establishing a short timeline, rather than distant deadlines for each project.

- ☐ 4. Analyze what you are good at and try to secure assignments that play to your strengths. Then, approach tasks with the confidence that you can successfully accomplish them.

- ☐ 5. Keep a daily "to-do" list and prioritize your duties into high, medium, and low. Do your most important tasks when your energy and attention level are highest. Do the next day's list before you leave work.

- ☐ 6. Minimize the amount of rework you do by trying to do things right the first time and by dealing with tasks on the spot. Clarify requirements to others so they get it right the first time.

- ☐ 7. Evaluate the value-added to every investment of your time and your employees' time: *Is this meeting necessary? Must this report be so long to meet the reader's needs? Is this form or added signature necessary?*

16

Development Plan Resources: Self-Direction

Build your expertise by reviewing the sources listed below:

Learning and Development Resources
Centrestar Academy. *Shaping performance expectations.* www.centrestar.com
Green, J. (2018). *The procrastination fix: 36 strategies proven to cure laziness and improve productivity: Daily training for mental toughness and self discipline.*
Hall, B. (2019). *Self-Discipline.*
Tracy, B. (2017). *Eat that frog! 21 great ways to stop procrastinating and get more done in less time.*

Be proactive and self-direct your career. Consider that reportedly, most bosses do not think about performance reviews, and that half of HR leaders do not believe the reviews are accurate.

16

Reflection and Application: Self-Direction

A person who is strong in self-direction is one who values continued learning, who looks for opportunities to improve, and who continually reflects on what they are doing well and what they can improve upon. As a leader you must devote time, energy, and planning to your development. Direct your life by creating a plan and then taking the steps necessary to put the plan into action.

Remember:

- Effective leadership requires that you be proactive.
- Kaizen: continually improve throughout your life.
- Be confident in your abilities and show that confidence to others.
- Be proactive. Look for areas that need improvement, situations that need to be changed, and people who will benefit from your direction. What other ways can you be proactive?

The most important concept I learned about this competency is:

_____

_____

_____

_____

_____

_____

_____

_____

_____

_____

_____

_____

_____

_____

_____

_____

_____

_____

_____

_____

_____

_____

_____

_____

16

To effectively apply this concept to my personal development I plan to:

16

_____

_____

_____

_____

_____

_____

_____

_____

_____

_____

_____

_____

_____

_____

_____

_____

_____

_____

_____

_____

You must choose your own path. But, learn from history.

COMPETENCY 17
Conflict Management

IMPORTANCE (I)	DEVELOPMENT NEED (DN)	VALUE (I x DN)
1 2 3 4 5	1 2 3 4 5	

Anticipates and seeks to resolve disagreements, complaints, and confrontations in a constructive manner.

Courage is what it takes to stand up and speak. Courage is also what it takes to sit down and listen.

– Winston Churchill[23]

When we think of conflict we tend to think of fighting. From arguments with your parents, to fights with your spouse, even to political strife and war, we think of conflict as being negative.

In the workplace healthy conflict can have a beneficial side while antagonistic conflict can build walls between people, tear teams apart, and make it difficult to get work done. Healthy conflict can lead to innovative ideas, increase creative energy, ferret out solutions to problems, and so much more.

The trick is to ensure that the conflict is healthy, and that unhealthy conflict is recognized early and neutralized. To do this you must realize that every leader has a particular conflict management style. Recognize what your style is, or better yet, know how to change your style to fit the situation. It is also crucial that you keep your emotions in check during conflict.

To clarify the concepts applicable to this competency, read the following list of observable and measurable knowledge, skills, tasks, and behaviors essential to all professionals:

✓ Anticipates and resolves conflicts, confrontations, and disagreements in a constructive manner.

✓ Addresses and seeks to resolve formal and informal complaints from employees.

✓ Maintains calm and does not respond emotionally to conflict situations.

17

✓ Recognizes conflict as an opportunity for growth and positive outcomes. Unafraid of healthy conflict.

Leadership Learning: Conflict Management

The Nature of Leadership

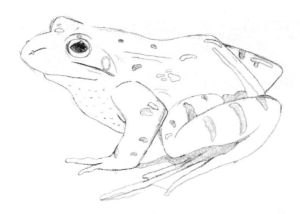

17

Frogs are masters at trying to avoid conflict.

You can learn amazing lessons from frogs (Smithsonian Channel, 2014), and specifically as related to conflict management. For example, the male hairy frog of the rainforest guards his eggs, protecting them for three weeks, and in doing so he sits motionless for days at a time. He is well adapted to this solitary, sentry task, having evolved skin tags, similar to hairs, on his back that collect oxygen from the water as he sits. If any creature dares to prey on him or his young, this amazing little frog can retract the skin of his fingertips to reveal claws made of sharp, solid bone. When threatened, he uses these to attack, which quickly puts an end to the conflict.

The gliding tree frog has a special ability for avoiding conflict. When threatened, this frog can escape quickly. He jumps into the air and spreads his webbed fingers like a parachute and glides to a safe place. Talk about avoiding conflict and landing on your feet!

The Darwin frog avoids conflict much like an opossum, by playing dead. Other frogs such as the Africa foam frog, work in teams. While most animals fight over mating, the foam frog is more concerned with species propagation than with simply passing on its own genes. Thus, many frogs come together to create a large nest that is fertilized with a variety of DNA.

The killer frog knows that being proactive is paramount. This frog can avoid disaster, such as drought, by going dormant underground. Once the frog emerges, he guards his tadpoles in a shallow pond, and even breaks down barriers to free his tadpoles into a larger pond if their small nursery begins to dry out.

Life as a frog involves a variety of conflicts. Some frogs decide that avoiding conflict is the best course of action, while others face conflict head on. At times it is best to avoid conflict, at other times it is better to engage and be proactive, and sometimes it is important to solicit teamwork and compromise. A true leader can assess a conflict situation and make an effective choice about how to manage it.

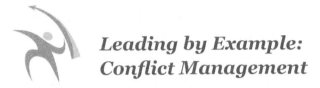 *Leading by Example: Conflict Management*

Real Life Leaders

Mary Robinson promoted compassion, nurturing, and listening.

Mary Robinson, the first female president of Ireland and a former United Nations high commissioner for human rights, once said, "Today's human rights violations are the causes of tomorrow's conflicts." In many ways, her goal was to manage conflict by heading it off before it had a chance to take hold. But when the situation called for it, this tough lady could also jump in and manage conflict.

Robinson believes that leading requires compassion, nurturing, and listening, as well as taking decisive action. By listening to the stories of others, she becomes informed and thus able to make better decisions. A trained barrister (lawyer) she was also able to advocate effectively for others. Invariably, Robinson used the right language and exceptional communication skills to resolve conflict and lead effectively.

17

Today, Robinson works with The Elders, an organization advocating for peace and human rights. She works tirelessly to end child marriage, stop war, support democracy, tackle climate change, and more. In her capacity as an Elder she visits many countries, working to bring leaders together to negotiate and advocate for a better world.

Assess Your Skills: Conflict Management

Take a moment to consider what you know about this concept and assess your skills. Indicate your level of agreement with each question.

How competent am I	Very little	Somewhat	Very much
Do I anticipate when conflict might arise?			
Do I have effective problem solving skills?			
Do I avoid negative confrontation and mitigate it when it occurs?			
Do I stay calm in the face of conflict?			
Can I recognize conflict as an opportunity for growth?			

7 Tips – What To Do: Conflict Management

The following tips will help you become more successful and continually improve your competence in this area. Check those that you need to develop.

☐ 1. Analyze your conflict management style. Do you avoid dealing with conflict, treat the problem superficially, use power, seek compromise, or use confrontation?

☐ 2. Realize that conflict is inevitable within most organizations. Learn how to manage it.

☐ 3. Talk to your colleagues and peers about your conflict management style. Recognize that not all organizations or departments will agree as to what conflict management style is preferred or most effective.

17

4. Deal with the root causes of conflict, not the symptoms. Determine whether the conflict is caused by differences in goals, competition for resources, failure in communication, misinterpretation of information, disagreement over standards, or incongruities in the organizational structure.

5. Engage in active listening to understand precisely what your counterpart's minimum requirement is in order to forge an agreement. Have people on each side of the conflict restate the other side's position.

6. Try to keep emotions out of the conflict. Resolve the issues in terms of value added to the organization, regardless of your feelings.

7. Take time to observe and learn about negotiation and conflict resolution processes and to analyze the factors that lead to resolution. Consult with others you respect in the organization to gain additional perspectives on the conflict.

Development Plan Resources: Conflict Management

Build your expertise by reviewing the sources listed below:

17

Learning and Development Resources
Centrestar Academy. *Responding to conflict in the workplace.* www.centrestar.com
Caspersen, D. & Elffers, J. (2015). *Changing the conversation: The 17 principles of conflict resolution.*
Gallo, A. (2017). *HBR guide to dealing with conflict.*
Mitchell, B. (2017). *The conflict resolution phrase book.*

Research indicates that managers may spend nearly half their time and energy dealing with conflict.

Reflection and Application: Conflict Management

As a leader you will sometimes find yourself in direct conflict with others. At other times you may find that you need to help other parties work through their conflict.

Remember:

- Look for the root cause of any conflict – what is really behind those emotions – not just the symptoms.

- Practice your listening skills to help you see both sides of the conflict, whether you are directly involved or simply helping others.

- Keep your emotions in check during conflict.

The most important concept I learned about this competency is:

_____

_____

_____

17

To effectively apply this concept to my personal development I plan to:

_____

_____

_____

_____

_____

_____

_____

_____

Conflict can have a positive outcome, when managed well.

COMPETENCY 18
Teamwork and Cooperation

IMPORTANCE (I)	DEVELOPMENT NEED (DN)	VALUE (I x DN)
1 2 3 4 5	1 2 3 4 5	

Demonstrates and fosters cooperation, communication, and consensus among individuals and groups.

You don't have to be a "person of influence" to be influential. In fact, the most influential people in my life are probably not even aware of the things they've taught me.

– Scott Adams[24]

Teamwork occurs when a group comes together to work toward a common goal. This happens in families, in society, and in the workplace. Sometimes it happens naturally, when people of similar ideas, desires, or traits decide to pursue something worthwhile together. This might happen in the workplace if a group decides, for example, to run a chili cook-off, collect money for a charity, or pursue a work-related goal.

In the workplace teams are built, that is, they are assembled (maybe randomly, but strategically is better) to accomplish a goal. In such situations, you will have a mix of people who may or may not care about the goal, who may or may not share common traits, who may or may not want to be on the team, or who may or may not get along.

No matter the purpose of the team or the thoughts and feelings of the people involved, as a leader your understanding of teamwork and cooperation is paramount to your success.

To clarify the concepts applicable to this competency, read the following list of observable and measurable knowledge, skills, tasks, and behaviors inherent to all professionals:

✓ Establishes teams and facilitates team development.

✓ Participates in team processes and activities. Is a team player.

✓ Fosters cooperation and teamwork.

18

✓ Establishes and promotes team goals, accountability, and rewards recognition.

✓ Creates an environment that encourages open communication and collective problem solving.

✓ Seeks consensus among diverse viewpoints to build group commitment.

Leadership Learning:
Teamwork and Cooperation

The Nature of Leadership

18

Wolves work as a team and will protect their pack no matter what.

Gray wolves work in packs to ensure survival. In fact, the wolf – native to North America and Eurasia – is possibly the most effective pack hunter in the world. Hunting in groups of six to twelve, they travel up to fifty miles a day in search of food. Surviving on small animals most of the time, they can also take on animals many times their size, such as bison, by working together.

Wolves work as a team to track prey, choosing a weak animal that is straggling behind a herd. Then, slowly and methodically they surround the creature, closing in, in a tighter and tighter formation, to keep the animal from escaping. Once the prey is trapped, the wolves attack as a group and secure their meal.

Wolves cooperate with each other in other ways as well. They rear their young together, bringing each other and the young food, and when necessary, protect one another.

The human world works much the same way, or at least it should. When people work together, they are capable of far more than they can accomplish individually. When working as a team, people build skyscrapers, create technology, and advance our world.

Leading by Example: Teamwork and Cooperation

Real Life Leaders

Abraham Lincoln promoted teamwork and cooperation, which was crucial to preserving the union.

Abraham Lincoln, the 16th President of the United States, was an incredible man. Although often riddled with self-doubt, Lincoln was a gifted speaker, and more importantly, Lincoln understood that teamwork and cooperation were crucial to preserving the great union of states. He dedicated his life toward achieving that goal.

In his famous Gettysburg Address of 1863, Lincoln asserted that, "Government of the people, by the people, for the people, shall not perish from the earth." He believed that the American form of government had to succeed, not only for the benefit of Americans, but to change the world for the better.

Reportedly, Lincoln's belief in teamwork, cooperation, and unity helped him lead the United States through the Civil War and emerge as a united nation. But it is important to stress that "Lincoln saw emancipation [the freeing of slaves] as a highly moral act, the one thing he thought he would be remembered for... he also saw the strategic value in it and helped convince others to support it." Lincoln knew how to leverage his knowledge and understanding to successfully keep the United States together.

18

Assess Your Skills:
Teamwork and Cooperation

Take a moment to consider what you know about this concept and assess your skills. Indicate your level of agreement with each question.

How competent am I	Very little	Somewhat	Very much
Do I appreciate the value of teamwork?			
How often do I demonstrate my commitment to teamwork?			
Do I foster cooperation and communication in my teams?			
How often do I initiate or participate in team activities?			
Do I recognize the stages of development groups often go through?			
Do I provide my teams the tools and resources they need to be successful?			

7 Tips – What To Do:
Teamwork and Cooperation

The following tips will help you become more successful and continually improve your competence in this area. Check those that you need to develop.

☐ 1. Ensure that group members understand the purpose of the team. Immediately after group formation, have each member identify the issues they consider to be the most important and suggest ways in which they can be resolved.

☐ 2. Recognize that teams go through phases. When assigning tasks, consider the phase the team is currently in.

☐ 3. Help team members decide how they will communicate within the group and how decisions will be reached.

☐ 4. Have the group leader specify the expectations of group members. Support team-building within the work unit, including training in interaction skills, group decision-making, active listening, and appreciating individual differences.

☐ 5. Give recognition to the team for team accomplishments and to individuals for individual contributions.

☐ 6. To promote teamwork, act as a role model by taking on any task that is necessary. Develop projects that use team members drawn from other areas in the organization as a way to foster organizational commitment and cooperation.

☐ 7. Examine benchmark or "best in class" work units in the organization and elsewhere and explore how they organize for success.

Development Plan Resources:
Teamwork and Cooperation

Build your expertise by reviewing the sources listed below:

Learning and Development Resources
Centrestar Academy. *Engaging in teamwork.* www.centrestar.com
Dungy, T. (2019). *The soul of a team: A modern day fable for winning teamwork.*
Maxwell, J.C. (2013). *The 17 indisputable laws of teamwork: Embrace them and empower your team.*
Sullivan, D. (2020). *Who not how: The formula to achieve bigger goals through accelerating teamwork.*

18

Teams do not come together by accident. Leaders must guide them through the stages of development.

Reflection and Application:
Teamwork and Cooperation

People say there is no "I" in team, but what does that mean? It means that when a team comes together, with a specific a goal in mind, it becomes "all for one and one for all." The good of the team is what matters, and accomplishing the goal is paramount.

Remember:

- Teams accomplish more than individuals accomplish on their own, and they do it more effectively and efficiently.

- Teamwork often leads to enhanced quality output.

- Working on a team, when done well, speeds things up by reducing learning (Lau, 2013) and dividing effort.

The most important concept I learned about this competency is:

_____

_____

_____

_____

_____

To effectively apply this concept to my personal development I plan to:

_____

_____

_____

_____

_____

_____

_____

_____

_____

18

Group decisions are typically better than individual decisions, which is to say that two heads are better than one.

COMPETENCY 19
Influencing and Negotiating

IMPORTANCE (I)	DEVELOPMENT NEED (DN)	VALUE (I x DN)
1 2 3 4 5	1 2 3 4 5	

Keeps groups and individuals informed; appropriately uses negotiation, persuasion, and authority in working with others to achieve goals; builds productive networks.

Questions are never indiscreet. Answers sometimes are.

– Oscar Wilde[25]

One definition of leadership is intentional influence (Grenny, 2012). Effective leaders work to influence the thinking and behavior of those they lead (Grenny, 2012). They do so through a combination of approaches, including thinking about the qualities they want to influence, role modeling behavior and attitudes they want to promote, talking to people about what needs to be done, and so on. An effective leader knows that just one of these approaches alone is insufficient to influence or create real change.

When it comes to negotiation, we often think of winning and losing. But effective negotiation involves both parties coming away feeling as though they have won. This type of negotiation creates bridges to future interactions.

To clarify the concepts applicable to this competency, read the following list of observable and measurable knowledge, skills, tasks, and behaviors essential to all professionals:

✓ Networks with key individuals or groups to achieve goals.

✓ Informs management, employees, and others of program objectives and developments.

✓ Promotes the organization or program to others.

✓ Identifies and understands the interests of others in the negotiation process.

✓ Negotiates and collaborates internally and externally to achieve group goals.

19

✓ Persuades management, employees, peers, and others to buy into a course of action.

✓ Uses power, authority, and influence appropriately to achieve goals.

Leadership Learning:
Influencing and Negotiating

The Nature of Leadership

Chickens practice hierarchical authority or "pecking order."

Chickens have a more complicated social network than may be apparent to casual observers. In fact, we get the commonly used term "pecking order" from the way that chickens and other fowl negotiate their relationships.

These little egg layers create entire societies with clear hierarchies, where some hens and roosters rise to the top and play roles of protector or provider. These high-level roles come with perks, including the ability to choose the best roosting spots, graze on the best feeding grounds first, and mate with the most desirable chickens. The pecking order keeps the hen house running smoothly. It lets young roosters know their place, keeps the females safe, and ensures that everyone gets along.

Chickens decide on the pecking order by strength and behavior. When a rooster wants to rule the roost he acts with confidence, crowing to assert his dominance, chasing away young roosters, and generally deciding how things will happen with the entire family. No one goes to bed or eats until the rooster says so. The hens also have

19

a hierarchy. The lead hen decides where the hens will roost and even decides if other hens can sit on their own eggs.

Canines also negotiate hierarchy. Typically, pack members defer to an alpha male who eats first, leads the pack where it will go, chooses who can eat what, decides where the pack will sleep, and so on. The term "top dog" likely derives from observations of canine hierarchies and leadership behaviors.

In the workplace, people influence one another and negotiate relationships and situations by displaying behaviors that exude confidence and that elicit respect or compliance. Of course, a leader needs employee buy-in. If people in the organization do not agree to follow, then one cannot lead.

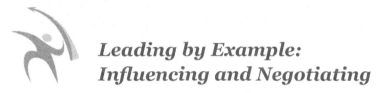

Leading by Example: Influencing and Negotiating

Real Life Leaders

Franklin and Eleanor Roosevelt influenced, negotiated, and promoted ideas through their fireside chats.

Franklin D. Roosevelt served as the President of the United States during one of the most challenging periods in history. He led not only through decisive action, but also through influence and negotiation. The only U.S. president to be elected four times, Roosevelt brought about a shift in American politics and social programs with his New Deal. He also helped lead the allied forces of Britain, the Soviet Union, and the United States to victory in World War II.

Confined to a wheelchair, one interesting way FDR influenced, negotiated, and promoted ideas was through his famous fireside chats. FDR faced many tough decisions, some of which he knew would be unpopular and difficult for people to understand. Roosevelt with the help of his wife Eleanor launched a series of thirty radio speeches where he explained his ideas and plans. Eventually the radio programs were dubbed "fireside chats" because they brought understanding and comfort to people.

The Roosevelts connected with the nation through their fireside chats. Eleanor Roosevelt was well known for positively leveraging her position as the first lady, as well as the media of the time. FRD was well known for his casual language to clearly explain issues and solutions which built support that helped get the country through the Great Depression and World War II. The heartfelt, personal language that FDR used united him with people and garnered support for his various campaigns. The Roosevelts' leadership by influence and negotiation is a consummate example of win-win.

Assess Your Skills:
Influencing and Negotiating

Take a moment to consider what you know about this concept and assess your skills. Indicate your level of agreement with each question.

How competent am I	Very little	Somewhat	Very much
Do I have a well-established network that I cultivate each day?			
Does my staff think I keep them informed and abreast of important issues?			
Are my negotiation skills effective?			
Do I understand how to work for win-win outcomes?			
Do I use my power and authority appropriately?			
Am I persuasive?			
Am I involved in industry associations?			

7 Tips – What To Do: Influencing and Negotiating

The following tips will help you become more successful and continually improve your competence in this area. Check those that you need to develop.

☐ 1. Join and be active in professional organizations and associations that complement your work and seek roles that provide visibility in those organizations.

☐ 2. Try to meet people outside your organization who hold positions like your own. Get together on a regular basis to trade ideas.

☐ 3. Monthly, circulate the highlights of recent activities in your department, including your objectives and the status of each.

☐ 4. When negotiating, do not place the other party in a position where they might lose face. Offer choices among alternatives. You can sometimes do this by following mild demands with stronger ones. Present a cooperative attitude.

☐ 5. Use active listening techniques to ensure that you understand the other person's point of view. Give the speaker your attention and listen carefully. Restate what the other person said. Ask questions to clarify the other's position. When people feel, you have listened to them, they are often more willing to listen to you, which helps keep conversations from escalating into an argument.

☐ 6. Ask your peers and subordinates for feedback with regard to how you use power, authority, and influence. You might ask the following questions: Am I fair? Do I back down too quickly? Do I avoid conflict? Do I come across too strongly? Do I always have to win?

☐ 7. Observe skilled negotiators in your organization. Ask them for advice with regard to using influence, persuasion, and achieving goals. Try to establish mentoring relationships with them.

19

Development Plan Resources:
Influencing and Negotiating

Build your expertise by reviewing the sources listed below:

Learning and Development Resources
Centrestar Academy. *Enhancing influence and negotiation skills.* www.centrestar.com
Cohan, A. (2017). *Influence without authority.*
Fisher, R. & Ury, W.L. (2011). *Getting to yes: Negotiating agreement without giving in.*
Voss, C. (2016). *Never split the difference: Negotiating as if your life depended on it.*

There are three elements involved in negotiation and influence: credibility, emotion, and logic.

19

Reflection and Application:
Influencing and Negotiating

An effective leader must influence those they lead. If you are well respected and confident, you are probably influencing people already. You must also influence and negotiate with those outside your area, such as customers, contractors, service providers, enforcement agents, the press, and competitors.

Remember:

- Effective leadership involves influencing others intentionally.
- Influence is not accomplished with a single silver bullet (Grenny, 2012). You must use various combinations of words and actions to influence others.
- You influence every day when you model behaviors.

The most important concept I learned about this competency is:

_____

_____

_____

_____

_____

_____

_____

_____

_____

_____

_____

_____

_____

_____

_____

_____

_____

_____

_____

_____

_____

_____

_____

19

To effectively apply this concept to my personal development I plan to:

_____

_____

_____

_____

_____

_____

_____

_____

_____

_____

_____

_____

19

_____

_____

_____

_____

_____

_____

_____

_____

_____

Always go for win-win.

Competency 20
Customer Focus

IMPORTANCE (I)	DEVELOPMENT NEED (DN)	VALUE (I x DN)
1 2 3 4 5	1 2 3 4 5	

Actively seeks customer input; ensures that customer needs are met; continually seeks to improve the quality of services, products, and processes.

Setting an example is not the main means of influencing others; it is the only means.

– Albert Einstein[26]

You might have heard that the customer is always right. Obviously, this is not correct. Sometimes a customer is wrong but pointing that out may result in losing the customer. The truth is, customers should always feel understood and appreciated. Even when a customer is wrong or demands something you cannot deliver, you must maintain a positive customer focus.

Remember that a single customer lost or dissatisfied is never just a single customer. Word of mouth travels fast, and negative words travel faster than positive ones. This is particularly true in today's world of social media. Always focus on customer needs: anticipate them, prepare for them, and meet them whenever possible.

20

To clarify the concepts applicable to this competency, read the following list of observable and measurable knowledge, skills, tasks, and behaviors essential to all professionals:

✓ Establishes and maintains a customer focus.

✓ Integrates customer needs and expectations into the development and delivery of services or products.

✓ Establishes and uses communication and feedback systems to ensure that customer requirements expectations are met.

✓ Continually seeks to improve the quality of services, products, and processes.

The Nature of Leadership

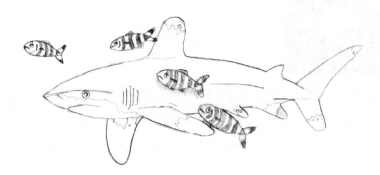

***Pilot fish, remora, and sharks have mutualistic roles that benefit each
other, which make them good role models for organizations.***

We often think of sharks as terrifying with those jaws and lifeless eyes, a monster on
the prowl. The truth, however, is that sharks simply want to eat and survive. Another
truth is that sharks are beneficial to other forms of ocean life, and sharks in turn
receive benefit from them.

As sharks swim they tend to pick up a few unwanted hitchhikers, such as parasites
and barnacles. Fortunately, shark cleaning services are available. Among them are
pilot fish and remora who want what the shark does not.

Pilot fish are small, meat eating fish. Their most efficient way of obtaining a meal
is to hang out around a shark and eat leftover scraps. In fact, a pilot fish will swim
into a shark's mouth to clean scraps stuck in its teeth. Sharks rarely feed on pilot
fish. Instead, the shark enjoys clean teeth as well as the fact that pilot fish also nip
barnacles and other parasites off the shark's sandpapery body. Pilot fish often travel
with the same shark, for days, weeks, even months, while keeping it clean.

Remora fish share a special relationship with sharks. Like pilot fish, remora eat
debris that sharks leave behind and they clean sharks of unwanted parasites. In
exchange, sharks offer the remora safety along with free meals. Remora also get a
free ride by attaching themselves to sharks using the suckers on top of their heads.

By maintaining customer focus, that is, by meeting the needs of pilot fish and
remora, sharks serve as mutualistic role models for businesses and organizations.

20

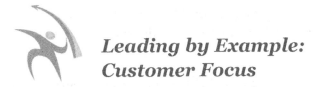

Leading by Example:
Customer Focus

Real Life Leaders

Horst Schulze made the Ritz Carlton famous for their legendary customer service while also and empowering employees.

You may have heard of Horst Schulze whose name is synonymous with the luxury hotel business. As president of The Ritz Carlton Hotels, he set the standard in the luxury hotel market. Today, he sets the standard for luxury in a new way as the leader of the Capella Hotel Group. The Ritz has always been associated with opulent hotels. The Capella Group is also a luxury experience for guests, but different, and that difference is attributable to Horst Schulze.

When Schulze was President of The Ritz, he realized that some luxury hotel customers wanted something different. He called that something "ultraluxury" (Forbes, 2012). Schulze meets the personal needs of guests in smaller hotels, which is how he structured the Capella hotels. Capella does not host conventions because the large spaces and large numbers of people are not conducive to the ultraluxury experience.

How has Schulze achieved world-class success in two such different settings? Because the business models are not the same, you might think that operationally the hotels are dissimilar as well. But it turns out that as far as customer service goes, they are very much the same. What both have in common is Horst Schulze's world-class focus on service.

The first thing to know is that Schulze built his success through researching the needs of the customer which oddly enough was what led him to Capella. Schulze

20

knew what The Ritz customers wanted, and for years he met those needs. Now Schulze knows what ultraluxury customers want, and he responds to those needs, as well.

Make a note of that and put a big star it. To provide the best in customer service, you must start by understanding what your customers want.

The second thing to know is that Schulze built his customer service systems not only to serve customers but also in a way that empowers his employees to be able to deliver outstanding customer service. If you think about it, you will see the reason is simple: People deliver customer service. Schultz built systems that support his employees in providing the level of service for which these hotels are famous. Write that down and factor it in next time you are faced with a decision about how to improve customer service in your organization.

Assess Your Skills: Customer Focus

Take a moment to consider what you know about this concept and assess your skills. Indicate your level of agreement with each question.

How competent am I	Very little	Somewhat	Very much
Do I have an appropriate focus on the needs of the customer?			
Do I actively research ever-changing client needs?			
Do I make it a priority to continually improve products, services, and staff?			
Am I aware of what other organizations in my industry are doing to serve their customers?			
Are effective communication systems a priority in my workplace?			

7 Tips – What To Do: Customer Focus

The following tips will help you become more successful and continually improve your competence in this area. Check those that you need to develop.

☐ 1. Use active listening techniques when communicating with customers. Take notes on conversations that are not documented in writing.

☐ 2. Consider the "bogus shopper" model, placing yourself in the role of an anonymous customer to gain knowledge about how a customer might see your organization.

☐ 3. Consider taking on employee assignments to better understand their jobs and how they interact with customers. Ensure that all employees understand that their efforts contribute to quality improvement. Include employees in the decision-making process so they feel responsibility for accomplishing goals and for customer satisfaction.

☐ 4. Conduct focus groups with internal and external customers to understand their needs. Make a point of receiving feedback on a regular basis from a sampling of your organization's customers.

☐ 5. Avoid introducing new work processes, services, or products without getting customer input in the design and development process.

☐ 6. Measure customer satisfaction on a regular basis to track improvements, reactions to changes in performance, and service delivery processes.

☐ 7. Study exemplary organizations to learn new techniques for measuring customer satisfaction.

Development Plan Resources: Customer Focus

20

Build your expertise by reviewing the sources listed below:

Learning and Development Resources

Centrestar Academy. *Promoting organizational focus on the customer.* www.centrestar.com

Cook, S. (2011). *Customer care excellence: How to create an effective customer focus.*

Manning, H. & Bodine, K. (2012). *Outside in: The power of putting customers at the center of your business.*

Morgan, B. (2019). *The customer of the future: 10 guiding principles for winning tomorrow's business.*

Organizations plan to differentiate themselves by offering exceptional service. Few achieve their goal.

Reflection and Application: Customer Focus

Customer focus means anticipating customer needs, communicating with them, and ensuring they are satisfied. Every person in your organization is a customer service professional. The attitudes and behaviors of each person, in some way, will impact customers. Train your employees to care about customers. Model customer focus.

Remember:

- The customer is not always right, but try to make sure the customer is satisfied.
- Word of mouth travels fast, especially the negative word.
- It is more cost effective to retain your current customers than to find new ones.
- Train your staff to be customer focused and give them the power to be able to do so.

The most important concept I learned in this competency is:

20

_____

_____

_____

To effectively apply this concept to my personal development I plan to:

_____

_____

_____

_____

_____

_____

The customer may not always be right but satisfying customer needs is the ultimate goal of your organization.

COMPETENCY 21
Interpersonal Relationship Building

IMPORTANCE (I)	DEVELOPMENT NEED (DN)	VALUE (I x DN)
1 2 3 4 5	1 2 3 4 5	

Considers and responds appropriately to the needs, feelings, and capabilities of others; seeks feedback and accurately assesses impact on others; provides helpful feedback; builds trust.

Whatever words we utter should be chosen with care for people will hear them and be influenced by them for good or ill.

– Buddha[27]

Life is about relationships. Unless you are a castaway living alone on a desert island you must build relationships to get along in the world, as well as to satisfy your own needs. This is true in both our personal and business lives. Networking has become a buzzword precisely because it has become essential. When you network you meet people and establish relationships. It is vital that you create these connections before you need to rely on them.

To clarify the concepts applicable to this competency, read the following list of observable and measurable knowledge, skills, tasks, and behaviors essential to all professionals:

✓ Considers and responds appropriately to the needs, feelings, and capabilities of others.

✓ Provides positive feedback in a manner that reinforces or elicits desirable behavior.

✓ Provides negative feedback in a constructive manner.

✓ Treats all colleagues in a fair and equitable manner.

✓ Creates a work environment where individuals are treated equitably.

✓ Considers individual interests and abilities in assigning work.

✓ Maintains a positive attitude and uses humor appropriately.

21

✓ Models patience, tolerance, enthusiasm, compassion, and empathy.

✓ Relates well to people regardless of position or background.

✓ Is approachable and available to colleagues and others.

✓ Demonstrates sincere concern and caring for people.

Leadership Learning:
Interpersonal Relationship Building

The Nature of Leadership

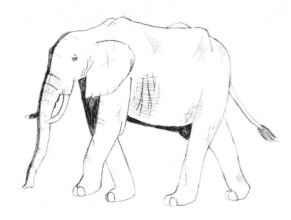

21

Elephants exhibit self-awareness and are social creatures who show emotions and have the ability to build relationships.

Many animals have complex social structures and develop unique interpersonal relationships. For example, elephants are social creatures. They comfort others who are upset or sad by offering caresses and little chirping sounds. They may do this to sooth to a herd-mate who is frightened or to comfort a mother who has lost her baby (Holland, 2015).

This type of interpersonal support – and relationship building – is also seen in many other animals, including some birds, apes, and dogs (Holland, 2015).

Leading by Example: Interpersonal Relationship Building

Real Life Leaders

Mother Teresa and Fred Rogers displayed an unforgettable devotion to teaching, supporting, and encouraging children and changed the world.

Building relationships during all stages of life is vitally important and few people exemplify the gold-standard for relationship building more than Mother Teresa. Known to millions across the globe, you would be hard-pressed to find anyone who had such an indelible impact on the lives of many children spanning multiple generations.

Mother Teresa's efforts were commemorated by museums, named churches, and even Albania's international airport is named after her. In 1979 she was honored with the Nobel Peace Prize and in 2017 named a co-patron of the Roman Catholic Archdiocese of Calcutta.

Fred Rogers from the television show Mister Rogers' Neighborhood, which was on the air for 33 years, was known for relationship building. Over the years, Fred Rogers earned the trust and respect of millions of children and their parents. Fred Rogers left an exemplary and long-lasting legacy due largely to his commitment to prioritizing the needs, feelings, and capabilities of children everywhere.

One example of his thoughtfulness and concern for others was when a young girl wrote him a letter asking about his pet goldfish. On one occasion Mr. Rogers mentioned that he was feeding his goldfish and while he regularly fed his fish

21

onscreen, he failed to articulate his actions. The young girl who voiced her concern was blind, and not privy to the fact that the fish was indeed being fed. As a result of this single letter, from that point on, every time he fed his pet goldfish Mr. Rogers verbally articulated as such.

Mr. Rogers was a true pioneer in early childhood development, with a relationship building presence unrivaled to this day. While his television show was mostly lighthearted and aimed at instilling the value of acceptance and kindness, he did not shy away from sensitive subjects like racism, and death [in particular the death of his pet goldfish] (King, 2019). By exploring these delicate topics in a caring and compassionate manner he further endeared himself to his many followers.

We may never see another Mr. Rogers in our lifetimes, but we can certainly strive to embody the characteristics he modeled. It is difficult to deny that the world would be a much better place if on occasion we all took the time to ask ourselves "What would Mr. Rogers do?"

Assess Your Skills: Interpersonal Relationship Building

Take a moment to consider what you know about this concept and assess your skills. Indicate your level of agreement with each question.

How competent am I	Very little	Somewhat	Very much
Am I aware of the needs and feelings of those around me?			
Do I set a positive example to my employees?			
Am I respected by those I work with?			
Do I treat others fairly and equally?			
Am I viewed as approachable?			
Do I have a positive attitude and sense of humor in the workplace?			
Do I provide feedback in a positive way that makes people want to improve?			

21

7 Tips – What To Do: Interpersonal Relationship Building

The following tips will help you become more successful and continually improve your competence in this area. Check those that you need to develop.

☐ 1. Consider having your work unit take an interpersonal styles inventory so that each member understands and develops a healthy respect for style differences within the group.

☐ 2. Demonstrate interest in your colleagues by using active listening techniques and responding positively.

☐ 3. Enjoy the diversity of dispositions and capabilities within your work unit. Capitalize on the diversity by devising ways to draw individuals into the work process.

☐ 4. Without engaging in preferential treatment or bending performance rules, show compassion by spending time with or listening to colleagues who experience personal difficulties. Also, listen to other points of view and try to understand them.

☐ 5. To the extent possible, establish expectations in writing and with specific measurable results that everyone can understand. When performance shortfalls occur, make sure that the responsible parties are held accountable. Have colleagues write down what they will be accountable for.

☐ 6. Encourage colleagues to come to you if they are treated unfairly. Have a suggestion box for those who hesitate to express concerns publicly.

☐ 7. Help colleagues deal realistically with business opportunities and personal qualifications and to translate these ideas into specific development plans. Always be enthusiastic about success.

21

Development Plan Resources: Interpersonal Relationship Building

Build your expertise by reviewing the sources listed below:

Learning and Development Resources
Centrestar Academy. *Interpersonal style profile: Analysis and interpretation; developing your client relationship advantage.* www.centrestar.com
Canales, B. (2019). *Enneagram in relationships: Understand your personality type and other personalities to build healthy relationships.*
Joy, M. (2020). *Getting relationships right: How to build resilience and thrive in life, love, and work.*
Tuhovsky, I. (2018). *The science of interpersonal relations.*

Most employees simply want to feel that they are appreciated by their supervisors.

Reflection and Application: Interpersonal Relationship Building

Work on building new relationships and strengthening existing relationships every day. Social media is a great way to turn even casual acquaintances into lasting relationships. Build relationships by being authentic. Show an interest in people and treat them well. Honesty, integrity, and friendliness are the foundation of authentic relationships.

Remember:

- Work to build relationships with those who lead you as well as with your stakeholders.
- Build authentic relationships with those you lead.
- Create an environment that promotes positive relationships.
- Model behaviors that build relationships including patience, acceptance, empathy, and humor.

The most important concept I learned about this competency is:

_____

_____

_____

_____

_____

_____

_____

_____

_____

_____

_____

_____

_____

_____

_____

_____

_____

_____

_____

_____

_____

_____

21

To effectively apply this concept to my personal development I plan to:

_____

_____

_____

_____

_____

_____

_____

_____

_____

_____

_____

_____

_____

21

_____

_____

_____

_____

_____

_____

_____

Networking – building relationships – must take place every day.

Competency Cluster D:
Organizational Leadership

Contrary to the opinion of many people, leaders are not born. Leaders are made, and they are made by effort and hard work.

– Vince Lombardi[28]

A key aspect of being an effective employer, supervisor, and leader is organizational leadership. This refers not only to leading your people, but also to leading your organization in fostering ideas and initiatives. It involves serving as a role model, sometimes coaching, but also directing efforts that grow the business and get results.

Here you will find descriptions for eleven competencies related to organizational leadership. These including **managing people**, **planning** and **evaluation**, **managing finances** and **budgets**, **managing technology**, **thinking creatively** and with **vision**, having **external awareness**, **strategic thinking** and **planning**, implementing **management controls,** valuing **diversity,** and **leading change**.

COMPETENCY 22
Human Performance Management

IMPORTANCE (I)	DEVELOPMENT NEED (DN)	VALUE (I x DN)
1 2 3 4 5	1 2 3 4 5	

Ensures effective systems for employee selection, placement, development, performance appraisal, recognition, and disciplinary action; promotes positive labor relations and employee well-being.

The superior man is easy to serve, but difficult to please. The inferior man is difficult to serve, but easy to please.

– Confucius[29]

Every leader, no matter the organization, must understand the human resources (HR) job function and the basics of human performance management. From writing job descriptions, interviewing, and hiring to conducting performance evaluations, all managers, supervisors, and leaders are involved with staffing and performance. These functions vary from organization to organization and depend to some extent on whether an organization has an HR department.

Leaders must have the ability to forecast the operational needs of their organizations in terms of human performance (Holmes, 2012). Managers must know to perform a job analysis to establish the skills and competencies required in every job for which they are responsible. They must also have a working understanding of job descriptions, as well as how to create those descriptions (Holmes, 2012).

Managers need access to a skills inventory tool to help them evaluate new and existing employees (Holmes, 2012). An example of a skills inventory is the Leadership Competency Inventory™ (LCI) in Section I: Plan Your Career. As a leader you must recognize the cost of employee turnover and strive to attract and retain the most qualified employees.

To clarify the concepts applicable to this competency, read the following list of observable and measurable knowledge, skills, tasks, and behaviors essential to all professionals:

✓ Plans for needed or mandated changes in the size and composition of staff.

✓ Takes an active role in recruiting and retaining staff.

22

✓ Exercises judgment within regulations when selecting for reassignment, promotions, and other routine employee actions.

✓ Determines needs and provides opportunities for employee orientation as well as for career development through counseling and training.

✓ Identifies performance expectations, assesses employee performance, gives timely feedback, and conducts formal performance appraisals.

✓ Recognizes and rewards performance based on standards and organizational goals.

✓ Takes appropriate corrective or disciplinary actions.

✓ Uses HR practices that further affirmative employment.

✓ Follows HR practices that promote good labor-management and employee relations.

✓ Supports programs and activities aimed at employee well-being such as safety, health, and family life.

Leadership Learning:
Human Performance Management

The Nature of Leadership

Geese manage performance by flying in a formation that rivals the best military fighter pilots.

The term "human performance management" often conjures images of elite athletes training to achieve their highest potential. But performance management is pertinent to everyone, in all walks of life, particularly in business environments. In the corporate realm human performance management entails: ensuring effective systems for employee selection, placement, development, performance appraisal, recognition, and disciplinary action; as well as promoting positive labor relations and employee well-being.

All these actions are crucial to ensuring an organization's employees (much like the afore mentioned athletes) are performing to their best capabilities. Some of the most effective ways in which these measures are achieved are through teamwork and communication. When we think of teamwork and communication, geese may not be the first things that come to mind. However, these amazing creatures have developed some phenomenal systems for increasing their performance by sticking together, communicating with, and looking out for each other.

Perhaps the greatest example of this is when they fly in a "V" formation. Using this method, they decrease energy expenditure, better track all the geese in their gaggle, and communicate more efficiently (Mirzaeinia, Heppner, & Hassanalian, (2020). Much like in human leadership, the pressure and exertion required for a goose to be "out front" can be overwhelming. Geese solve this problem by rotating the "leaders" of the gaggle to the back of the formation on a regular basis.

Although alternating positions within a corporation may not be a suitable option, many leaders would benefit from the occasional lessening of their responsibilities. That is one reason for making sure that your subordinates are well-trained, capable, and executing their duties as best they can.

Leading by Example:
Human Performance Management

Real Life Leaders

Anne Sullivan, a tutor who had the ability to truly see and understand another person's perspective. achieved remarkable results.

In 1887, 21-year-old Anne Sullivan was sent to tutor an isolated, frustrated, and angry 7-year-old Helen Keller. Keller was blind and deaf after having scarlet fever as a baby, and because of her behavior, no school for the blind would accept her.

You may have seen the movie The Miracle Worker, which describes the struggle her tutors endured before Keller first understood the concept of language and could use language to communicate with the world. Once she achieved this, Sullivan taught Keller to read and write, and the pair continued to work successfully together. Thanks to Anne Sullivan's compassion and patience, Keller went on to be one of the most accomplished women of the twentieth century.

What talents or skills did Sullivan have that gave her the wherewithal to achieve such an amazing feat? You may assume she had every advantage and a quality education, but she did not. Sullivan was born into a poor family, and at 5-years-old she contracted a bacterial eye infection that left her nearly blind. Three years later, she lost her mother. Her father sent her and her brother to a poorhouse. Her brother died there, but Anne Sullivan had a bit of luck. In 1880, when she was 14, Sullivan was sent to the Perkins School for the Blind. There she learned to read and write; however, she had no training as a teacher.

One apparent reason for Sullivan's success was her tenacity in it. But the question is how did Sullivan forge a connection fighting to communicate with Keller. Sullivan never quit. But the question is how did Sullivan forge a connection, a connection that allowed her to build a relationship with a seemingly uncontrollable child? All leaders know the difficulty of making genuine connections, even in the best of circumstances, and yet Sullivan's circumstances could hardly have been more challenging.

Howard Gardner (Gardner, 2006) named Sullivan as an example of an interpersonal genius and said it was those interpersonal skills – her ability to truly see and understand another person – that contributed to her success with Helen Keller. Few of us can claim to be interpersonal geniuses, but we can take a lesson from Anne Sullivan. To be effective, think not only about what you know, but also about how you relate to others.

Assess Your Skills:
Human Performance Management

Take a moment to consider what you know about this concept and assess your skills. Indicate your level of agreement with each question.

How competent am I	Very little	Somewhat	Very much
Do I know my staff well?			
Do I understand the needs of my staff, personally and professionally?			
Is the safety of my staff a top priority?			
Do I take an active role in recruiting?			
Do I work on training, coaching, and performance evaluation every day?			
Does each member of my team know what I expect of them?			
Do I provide recognition to my staff for a job well done?			
Do I know how to take appropriate disciplinary action when performance issues arise?			

7 Tips – What To Do: Human Performance Management

The following tips will help you become more successful and continually improve your competence in this area. Check those that you need to develop.

☐ 1. Recognize and assess internal and external factors that will influence the need for and availability of competent employees in the near and long-term future. Consider: Expansion or downsizing plans, expected turnover, expected changes in technology, economic forecasts.

☐ 2. Plan for new employee needs and start the recruiting process before the job is available. Define and write job descriptions for all the jobs in your department. Include required knowledge, skills, and abilities.

☐ 3. Considering the goals of your unit and the mix of talent that would best serve these goals, what talents do you most need to attract into your unit in the future? Set up a timeline for those human resource needs.

☐ 4. When new personnel arrive, implement a structured orientation process for the first few months. Use others to help in the orientation. Establish follow-up processes to keep the orientation process on track.

22

5. Facilitate developmental assignments for new and seasoned employees to enhance performance and on the job growth. Use job rotations to develop multiple-technology capabilities across jobs, which will provide solid training and development experience.

6. Stay up-to-date on career opportunities, training programs, and developmental assignments that are available in your organization and in sister organizations.

7. If employees consistently experience performance problems or fall short of goals, analyze the root causes. Offer assistance and solutions. Use an employee assistance program, or use outside counseling for more challenging cases.

Development Plan Resources: Human Performance Management

Build your expertise by reviewing the sources listed below:

Learning and Development Resources
Centrestar Academy. *Coaching for exemplary performance.* www.centrestar.com
Colan, L.J. (2017). *The 5 coaching habits of excellent leaders.*
Conklin, T. (2019). *The 5 principles of human performance.*
Throness, T. (2017). *Power of people skills: how to eliminate 90% of your hr problems and dramatically increase team and company morale and performance. Organizations: a strategic approach.*

Output of exemplary employees can be five to ten times higher than that of the average employee.

Reflection and Application:
Human Performance Management

Managing the performance of those on your team is an important part of your leadership duties. Even if you have an HR department who handles much of the hiring and discipline, you must still be knowledgeable and informed.

Remember:

- You need access to a skills inventory to assess the skills of new hires and to evaluate the performance of current employees. For leadership positions, you can use this book.

- Job descriptions are a critical part of hiring and performance appraisals.

- Hiring usually costs more than training and coaching an existing employee.

The most important concept I learned about this competency is:

_____

_____

_____

_____

_____

_____

_____

_____

_____

_____

_____

_____

_____

_____

22

To effectively apply this concept to my personal development I plan to:

22

Employees who feel valued perform better.

COMPETENCY 23
Planning and Evaluation

IMPORTANCE (I)	DEVELOPMENT NEED (DN)	VALUE (I x DN)
1 2 3 4 5	1 2 3 4 5	

Establishes policies, guidelines, plans and priorities; plans and coordinates with others; aligns required resources; monitors progress and evaluates outcomes; improves organizational efficiency and effectiveness.

A goal without a plan is just a wish.

– Antoine de Saint-Exupery[30]

A famous book says the best laid plans of mice and men often go awry (Steinbeck, 1937). However, planning is still a fundamental aspect of leadership. While plans do not always unfold as you intend, planning gives you a place to start, a logical way to work towards your goals, and a yard stick by which to measure success. It is also true that planning is only as productive as your dedication to following through with your plan.

Planning involves more than one activity. It begins when you create your list of goals. Then you define the incremental steps you must take toward achieving each goal. Next, you execute your plans to take each step and reach each goal. Finally, you review what worked and learn lessons from what did not work well.

To clarify the concepts applicable to this competency, read the following list of observable and measurable knowledge, skills, tasks, and behaviors essential to all professionals:

23

- ✓ Establishes policies or guidelines for the organization or program area.
- ✓ Sets priorities and coordinates work of the staff to meet goals.
- ✓ Ensures that activities, services, and products meet organizational mission, management policies, and customer needs.
- ✓ Identifies, obtains, and uses the resources required to meet objectives.
- ✓ Coordinates with other parts of the organization to accomplish goals.

✓ Identifies how organizational or program results will be measured.

✓ Monitors programs and activities to assure that discrepancies are identified and corrected as necessary.

✓ Participates in the evaluation of program and project accomplishments.

✓ Contributes to improving organizational and program efficiency and effectiveness.

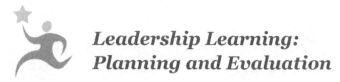

Leadership Learning: Planning and Evaluation

The Nature of Leadership

23

Squirrels plan their time, stockpile food, and evaluate situations to thwart predators.

Whether you are a student writing a book report, a CEO of a *Fortune* 500 company, or president of a nation, planning is fundamental. Even bushy tailed squirrels plan ahead, evaluate the weather and the season, and take action.

Imagine that you live in a hole in a tree. The sun is shining, the birds are singing, and you are chewing on an acorn, currently fat and happy. What do you do next? Do you watch the clouds go by and do nothing? Do you play a game of tag and have fun? Not if you are a squirrel.

Squirrels plan their time, and so their future, by gathering and saving nuts for the winter. During the warm summer months squirrels spend considerable time finding or creating a home and hunting for and gathering food within the three or four acres they call home. They then binge-eat, but they also hide away nuts for the winter.

Stockpiling food is an essential part of squirrel life. They find nuts and bury them a few inches under the ground. In the cold months they sniff out the nuts, even through inches of snow, and dig them up for nutritious meals.

By planning and by executing their plans well, squirrels live through even the most severe winters. People need to do same: Think ahead and plan. Carry out the plan. Evaluate the results.

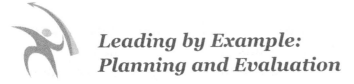

Leading by Example: Planning and Evaluation

Real Life Leaders

Susan B. Anthony fought for women's rights and became known as the voice for equality.

23

In 1920, women in America won the right to vote, affording them the ability to not only amplify their voices but giving rise to a new era of women's liberation. One of the spearheads in this fight for fairness was Susan B. Anthony. Although she did not live long enough to see the fruits of her labor in the form of voting equality, her work as President of the National Woman Suffrage Association helped pave the way for today's modern women and solidified her as the voice of women's equality (Barry, 2020).

This right for women to vote was not easily won. This effort took tremendous planning, coordination, resources, and prioritization, all of which were personified by Susan B. Anthony and her suffragettes. The planning and evaluation involved in bringing the 19th Amendment of the Constitution to light was nothing short of phenomenal.

Anthony was a true visionary leader. Her ability to coordinate with others; procure and distribute the necessary resources; monitor progress and evaluating outcomes; improve organization efficiency and effectiveness to bring attention to and further the women's rights movement was unparalleled. In a time when women were not considered equal to men, she showed the world that women were not only capable of leading but excelled at it.

Her speeches roused the masses and lit a fire that is still burns today. One hundred years after women won the right to vote, Americans saw their first female Vice-President in Kamala Harris, a victory that would not have been possible without the efforts of Susan B. Anthony, thus proving that exemplary planning, evaluation, and execution can have long-lasting, life-changing effects.

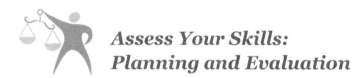

Assess Your Skills: Planning and Evaluation

Take a moment to consider what you know about this concept and assess your skills. Indicate your level of agreement with each question.

How competent am I	Very little	Somewhat	Very much
Do I set priorities and coordinate activities to meet them?			
When I set priorities and goals, do they support the organizational mission and vision?			
Are customer needs part of my planning?			
Do I regularly evaluate employee performance?			
Am I consistent in evaluating the results of my own actions?			
Do my actions contribute to efficiency in the workplace?			

23

7 Tips – What To Do:
Planning and Evaluation

The following tips will help you become more successful and continually improve your competence in this area. Check those that you need to develop.

☐ 1. Formulate operational plans: define goals and objectives; structure the organization in a way to achieve your goals and objectives; assign responsibilities; allocate resources; encourage awareness of potential problems.

☐ 2. Examine the performance of best-in-class work units to understand their success. Benchmark similar organizational units within and outside of your organizational area to understand how they measure performance.

☐ 3. Go to seminars and lectures inside and outside of your organization to familiarize yourself with trends that may affect the future work of your unit. Observe proficient cross-functional team leaders and understand what they do to get the job done.

☐ 4. Develop annual goals, specify interim goals and due dates, and each month revisit the goals to assess accomplishments. Establish a project management system that will alert you to missed interim dates and deadlines.

☐ 5. For each of your unit's goals, develop a detailed plan through consultation with others that specifies how the goal will be accomplished, by when, and the resources needed to make it happen.

☐ 6. Continually evaluate how well your organizational area is doing in achieving its objectives. Have regular meetings to keep people informed.

☐ 7. Use a communication method such as a highly visible bulletin or white board and list objectives and accomplishments toward meeting those objectives. Keep in mind that planning, controlling, evaluation, and feedback are a cycle of activities.

23

Development Plan Resources: Planning and Evaluation

Build your expertise by reviewing the sources listed below:

Learning and Development Resources
Centrestar Academy. *Defining and planning projects.* www.centrestar.com
Portny, S.E. (2020). *Project management for dummies.*
Project Management Institute (PMI). (2021). *A guide to the project management body of knowledge: PMBOK(R) Guide.*
Stevens, A. (2013). *Turn your dreams and wants into achievable SMART goals!: A comprehensive manual on effective goal-setting.*

Remember these sayings: You never have time to do it right, but you always have time to do it over; An ounce of prevention is worth a pound of cure.

Reflection and Application: Planning and Evaluation

Planning is vital to improving workplace processes, including establishing policies and priorities, setting and achieving goals, procuring and utilizing resources, serving customers, hiring employees, and negotiating change, both internal and external.

Remember:

- Planning is a necessary part of accomplishing goals.
- Of course, circumstances change, and plans do not always unfold the way you thought they would. Sometimes you need to be flexible and change the plan on the fly.
- Perhaps the most important part of a plan is evaluating how successful the plan was and learning lessons for the future.

23

The most important concept I learned about this competency is:

_____

_____

_____

_____

_____

_____

_____

_____

_____

_____

_____

_____

_____

_____

_____

_____

_____

_____

_____

_____

_____

_____

_____

_____

23

To effectively apply this concept to my personal development I plan to:

23

Every successful project begins with a plan.

COMPETENCY 24
Financial Management and Budgeting

IMPORTANCE (I)	DEVELOPMENT NEED (DN)	VALUE (I x DN)
1 2 3 4 5	1 2 3 4 5	

Understands budget process; prepares and justifies budgets; monitors expenses; manages profit/loss ratios as appropriate.

You need to understand the difference between an asset and a liability. An asset puts money in your pocket and a liability takes money from your pocket. The rich understand the difference and buy assets, not liabilities.

– Robert Kiyosaki[31]

Effective management includes the ability to manage finances and create budgets. Successful leaders know how to read a variety of financial statements, as well as how to create them. They can read, evaluate, develop, and approve budgets. They also know how to bring multiple team or project budgets into a larger budget.

When it comes to budgeting and finances, you must know when to spend money in order to earn money. Thus, a productive leader knows how to justify budget expenditures and anticipate future needs.

To clarify the concepts applicable to this competency, read the following list of observable and measurable knowledge, skills, tasks, and behaviors essential to all professionals, no matter your industry:

24

✓ Prepares budgets for own organization, projects, and activities.

✓ Applies an understanding of the roles and functions of diverse groups in the budget process.

✓ Explains or justifies budget requests.

✓ Tracks expenses and monitors budget to ensure cost-effective resource management.

✓ Oversees or participates in the procurement of equipment, facilities, supplies, and services.

✓ Monitors work done by contractors or grantees.

✓ Fosters an environment where cost benefit ratios are continually improved.

Leadership Learning: Financial Management and Budgeting

The Nature of Leadership

Artic animals budget their time, conserve energy, and prepare for winter.

Previously, we discussed how squirrels allocate food for the winter. This is a type of budgeting. While animals do not budget money, they know how to budget resources.

Budgeting resources correctly is key to survival for animals living in the arctic tundra, as well. These animals have adapted to life in a harsh environment. Some animals grow a new coat of fur in the fall to help them blend in better with snow and sparse vegetation (ASU, n.d.). All artic animals budget their time, managing when to eat and when to sleep.

Many artic animals learn to eat at night to avoid predators (ASU, n.d.). They also hibernate during extreme cold, choosing to reserve their energy until food and warmth are more readily available. But to survive hibernation, they must build fat reserves by gorging themselves on food in the fall and early winter. Fortunately, long days on the tundra provide adequate time for animals to forage, hunt, and eat, allowing them the time to prepare for winter.

Whether you are an animal preparing for the coming cold, a parent preparing for their child's future, or a businessperson expecting to land a deal, budgeting your time, energy, money, and other resources is vital to your success.

Leading by Example:
Financial Management and Budgeting

Real Life Leaders

Lee Iacocca's ingenuity and smart money decisions made the Chrysler company competitive.

When it comes to financial management and budgeting, some CEOs fail, while others are exceptionally successful. One example that stands out is Lido, "Lee," Iacocca, CEO of Chrysler Corporation from 1979 through the early 1990s. Acknowledged as one of the greatest leaders of all time by *Portfolio Magazine*, his name appears on many great leader lists, and for good reason. His ingenuity, tenacity, and financial management abilities led Chrysler through an exceptionally difficult time in the late 1970s when the company was on the verge of bankruptcy amid a series of bad decisions that led to automotive recalls.

He rescued the failing auto maker with ingenuity and smart money decisions. To secure the necessary money, Lee Iacocca went to the U.S. Congress to get the first big auto maker bailout in history – a loan guarantee that helped fund a variety of new initiatives.

For inspiration, Iacocca looked to his past and to the needs of his customers. He saw that people needed small, affordable cars, but also that Asia was on to something in the way of the minivan. Iacocca pulled a couple of designs from his days at Ford – designs that were nixed early in the design phase – and pushed them through at Chrysler. This led to the Chrysler K car, the Dodge Caravan, Chrysler Horizon, and others – all big money makers.

24

Through the combination of accessing funding, budgeting those funds, and directing them to projects, Iacocca led Chrysler into a successful run throughout the 1980s and 1990s.

Assess Your Skills:
Financial Management and Budgeting

Take a moment to consider what you know about this concept and assess your skills. Indicate your level of agreement with each question.

How competent am I	Very little	Somewhat	Very much
Am I adept a preparing budgets and estimates?			
Do I understand the roles of various groups and inputs in the budgeting process?			
Are my work units organized to be cost effective and productive?			
Can I justify my budget requests and expenditures?			
Do I personally oversee procurement of major equipment and purchases?			
In my workplace, is work done by contractors effectively supervised?			

7 Tips – What To Do:
Financial Management and Budgeting

The following tips will help you become more successful and continually improve your competence in this area. Check those that you need to develop.

☐ 1. Use budget development as an opportunity for constructive communication and debate, and coordinate with others during the process.

☐ 2. Involve key colleagues in budget development, and ensure that they are aware of the costs associated with their work.

☐ 3. Seek out a financial expert within your organization. Ask for help when you have questions. Visit organizations known for excellence in areas like yours.

24

4. Develop an in-depth understanding of your organization's budget by reviewing each line in the budget, and talk to those responsible for resource requests.

5. Compare ratios of a current time period with those of the past. Gauge improvement. Review budget items to understand the reason for any discrepancy. Contact suppliers to jointly solve problems and eliminate excess costs.

6. Benchmark financial tracking processes against those in other organizations to identify opportunities for improvement. Measure key cost-effectiveness indicators and compare them with similar units.

7. Delegate responsibility for monitoring various financial outlays to appropriate individuals, and ensure that they develop expertise in their areas.

Development Plan Resources: Financial Management and Budgeting

Build your expertise by reviewing the sources listed below:

Learning and Development Resources
Centrestar Academy. *Examining Financial Knowledge Essentials.* www.centrestar.com
Berman, K. (2013). *Financial intelligence: A manager's guide to knowing what the numbers really mean.*
Knight, J. & Thomas, R. (2012). *Project management for profit: A failsafe guide to keeping projects on track and on budget.*
Siciliano, G. (2014). *Finance for nonfinancial managers.*

24

**Finance is the language of business.
Remember: no money, no mission.**

Reflection and Application: Financial Management and Budgeting

As a leader you must develop your financial management skills. This means understanding the technology necessary to manage finances in your organization. It also means being knowledgeable about the state of financial management related technology and various costs associated with your industry.

Remember:

- You must justify, which means to provide a business reason and prove the value for, every line item on your budget.

- Forward-thinking leaders anticipate the needs of their team when budgeting.

- Budget-savvy leaders teach their teams to manage organizational finances effectively.

The most important concept I learned about this competency is:

_____

_____

_____

To effectively apply this concept to my personal development I plan to:

_____

_____

_____

_____

_____

_____

_____

_____

24

Well-constructed budgets save money.

Competency 25
Technology Management

IMPORTANCE (I)	DEVELOPMENT NEED (DN)	VALUE (I x DN)
1 2 3 4 5	1 2 3 4 5	

Stays informed about new technology; applies new technologies to organizational needs; ensures staff is trained and able to use technology required for the job.

Success is a lousy teacher. It seduces smart people into thinking they can't lose.

— Bill Gates[32]

When we think about leadership, we often think first about managing people and relationships. But managing technology is also central to leadership. Managing new technologies is a crucial skill in our modern era, since something new seems to happen every day. One way to stay current is to determine who can educate and advise you on new technology as it applies to the needs of your organization

As you manage existing technologies in your organization, be sure to stay abreast of changing best practices, and train your team on the latest technological efficiencies and procedures.

Set goals for integrating new technology into your workplace and keep in mind there will often be a learning curve. You must allow time for your team to become proficient in new technologies.

To clarify the concepts applicable to this competency, read the following list of observable and measurable knowledge, skills, tasks, and behaviors essential to all professionals:

✓ Encourages staff to stay current and informed about technological changes, scientific research, and automation.

✓ Applies evolving technologies and methodologies to organizational needs.

✓ Makes certain that staff are trained and capable in using new technology.

25

Leadership Learning:
Technology Management

The Nature of Leadership

Giant Anteaters use their body length of over two meters to reach deeply into ant hills.

Just a few generations ago humans were without telephones, automobiles, even electricity. Over time, however, we created these tools to better manage our lives, and Mother Nature has supported animals in their evolution as well.

The giant anteater for example has a body length that averages over two meters. It has a long, sticky tongue that it uses as a dinner delivery system. The anteater finds a hole filled with ants, then sticks its tongue in and enjoys a veritable buffet.

Another example is the peppered moth, which a hundred years ago was mostly white, with black peppered spots. Then, little by little, these moths became darker and darker. Today, most of them – as many as 95 percent – are a deep gray with black peppering ("8 Examples," 2011). Exactly why this occurred is up for debate, however it has been suggested that more dark rocks and buildings of today made the difference, perhaps because of pollution.

The New England blue mussel is another example of managing one's technological capability due to changing situations ("8 Examples", 2011). As the Asian shore crab invaded New England waters and began eating blue mussels, the mussels adapted. When muscles sense Asian shore crabs in their vicinity, they thicken their shells for protection ("8 Examples", 2011). Muscles from other areas who have not been exposed to Asian crabs do not thicken their shells ("8 Examples", 2011); they have not needed to adapt.

Over millennia, animals have adapted to their worlds. Leaders must do the same. Leaders must continually adapt by understanding what technology can do for their organizations, and they must learn how to use technology to the best advantage.

25

Leading by Example:
Technology Management

Real Life Leaders

Larry Page nurtures new technologies at Google.

As co-founder of Internet giant Google, Larry Page knows a thing or two about change and how to manage technology. In many ways, Page could be considered the poster child for technological change.

As one Business Insider article put it, Page does not focus on how to beat the competition, instead, he focuses on, "transforming products and services completely" (Nisen, 2013). From the beginning, Page has broken technological glass ceilings, anticipated customer needs, and created not only new devices and services, but in the process has created new customer needs as well. In so doing, Page thoroughly understands technology management, and knows how to nurture and push his employees in a way that supports the use of new technologies.

25

A somewhat telling joke around Google office goes like this: A brainiac who works in the lab walks into Page's office one day wielding his latest world-changing invention — a time machine. As the scientist reaches for the power cord to begin a demo, Page fires off a powerful question: "Why do you need to plug it in?" (As cited in Helft, 2014).

Assess Your Skills:
Technology Management

Take a moment to consider what you know about this concept and assess your skills. Indicate your level of agreement with each question.

How competent am I	Very little	Somewhat	Very much
Is my team technically competent?			
Do I ensure adequate training of all my staff?			
Do I identify training needs and arrange for technology education for those I supervise?			
Do I encourage my staff to stay current on technologies in their area through my word and actions?			
How well do I apply technology to meet changing organizational needs?			

7 Tips – What To Do:
Technology Management

The following tips will help you become more successful and continually improve your competence in this area. Check those that you need to develop.

☐ 1. First, do you need state-of-the-art technology? Would the benefits outweigh the cost? Can you introduce new technology successfully? Second, evaluate the technological competence of your team members. Consider, rotating employees so all are cross-trained.

☐ 2. Provide training programs for new technologies. Send staff to vendor shows to stay abreast of technology developments.

☐ 3. Stay current with technology by reading relevant magazines, journals, and electronic bulletin boards, and subscribe to technical magazines and journals. Ask employees to peruse publications, take note of articles that apply to their work, and circulate the articles to appropriate employees.

☐ 4. Encourage your team to network with employees in other areas. Participate in professional technological organizations. Improve processes through assessment and feedback.

25

5. Network with other leaders and exchange ideas relevant to technical advances in your field. Display a willingness to use new technology in your work.

6. Nurture relationships with individuals in outside organizations who are introducing new technology and advancements. Note any opportunities that could help your work.

7. Search for vendors who will make presentations to your employees. Compile a list of resources in technical subjects. To implement a new technology, you must plan its introduction and assess training needs, and have a strategy of defect management and prevention.

Development Plan Resources: Technology Management

Build your expertise by reviewing the sources listed below:

Learning and Development Resources
Centrestar Academy. *Supporting innovation by applying SBIR Phase III commercialization practices.* www.centrestar.com
Donahue, W. (2021). Unlocking Lean Six Sigma.
Fournier, C. (2017). *The manager's path: a guide for tech leaders navigating growth and change.*
Roser, C, (2021). *All about pull production: designing, implementing, and maintaining kanban, conwip, and other pull systems in lean production.*

A pathway to accelerate the commercialization of technology is through collaboration with established private sector organizations.

25

Reflection and Application: Technology Management

Managing technology involves not only choosing and implementing the right technologies, but also being a well-informed resource for those who need help.

Remember:

- Attend training and read literature on new technologies yourself so that you have at least a functional knowledge of the technological applications relevant to your area.

- Encourage team leaders to read manuals and attend necessary training.

- Post important warnings and make operational manuals accessible to all employees.

The most important concept I learned about this competency is:

_____

_____

_____

To effectively apply this concept to my personal development I plan to:

_____

_____

_____

_____

_____

_____

_____

_____

25

Technology is vital to helping people live better lives.

COMPETENCY 26
Creative Thinking

IMPORTANCE (I)	DEVELOPMENT NEED (DN)	VALUE (I x DN)
1 2 3 4 5	1 2 3 4 5	

Develops new insights and novel solutions; embraces innovations and fosters innovative thinking in others.

Don't live life anyhow, else you get anywhere. Plan your life somehow and you can get somewhere. A slow plan is better than no plan.

– Israelmore Ayivor[33]

Thinking creatively is not just the purview of inventors, designers, engineers, and architects; creative thinking is a necessary quality of all leaders. Through creative thinking we are better able to anticipate issues and opportunities, bring diverse mindsets and ideas into a cohesive plan, prepare for new and developing technologies, and innovate in ways that allows organizations to rise and be noticed.

Some people feel that they are not capable of creative thinking, but this is not true. Anyone can learn to think creatively as long as they are given plenty of time and opportunity.

To clarify the concepts applicable to this competency, read the following list of observable and measurable knowledge, skills, tasks, and behaviors essential to all professionals:

26

✓ Develops insights into situations and applies innovative solutions to make improvements.

✓ Creates an environment that encourages employees to be inventive, imaginative, and resourceful.

✓ Stimulates nontraditional approaches to tasks and assignments.

✓ Synthesizes diverse information, suggestions, and solutions into innovative approaches.

Leadership Learning: Creative Thinking

The Nature of Leadership

Crows are crafty and skilled at creative problem solving.

People say that one thing which separates man from animals is our creative mind. Yet many animals express creative abilities as well. For example, rats, eagles, and the great apes use creativity to construct shelter. Dogs are notorious for using creativity to manipulate their humans to perform, such as when they allow a ball to roll under a piece of furniture, so humans must retrieve it.

Many experiments show how animals use creativity to solve problems. One involves the crow. An experimenter dropped a piece of food down a cylinder beyond a crow's reach (Creative Commons, 2009). The crow was given a length of wire such as a straightened-out paper clip. After spending several minutes jamming the straight wire into the cylinder with no success, the crow got an idea. She took the wire, stepped off to the side, bent a hook into the end of the wire, re-inserted the wire into the cylinder, and instantly hooked the food and brought it out. Creativity. Ingenuity. Amazing.

People use creativity to solve problems every day, even to change their moods or simply to look at something from another perspective. One mother accidentally put liquid dish soap into the automatic dishwater. Bubble mania, similar to what one might expect on a silly television show, ensued with bubbles pouring out of the appliance and covering the kitchen floor while her two-year-old son looked on.

While some parents might have quickly ushered the child away, and hurriedly cleaned up the mess, this mother had a creative idea. She allowed her child to enjoy

26

playing in the bubbles while she grabbed a rag and used the bubbles to wipe the cabinet fronts, which needed a good cleaning anyway.

After some playing and cleaning, and delightful laughter from the toddler, the bubbles were mostly gone, the kitchen was cleaner, and both child and mother were in good spirits.

Sometimes creative thinking lets you turn failure into an opportunity. They say that life is 5 percent what happens to you and 95 percent how you react to it. Be creative in how you handle things, particularly adversity, and you will find more success and joy in life.

Leading by Example:
Creative Thinking

Real Life Leaders

George Washington surprised the British with his creative thinking on Christmas Eve.

In 1776, the American Revolutionary War against the British was not going well. The Americans had lost many battles. The overlords felt emboldened and the rebels felt defeated. But George Washington had an idea to change all that. Washington thought his men needed a morale boost, something to give them a sense of victory and hope, and to encourage new men to take up the fight.

Thus, on December 25, 1776, Washington and an army of men crossed the Delaware River with a plan to surprise the British and deal them a shocking blow. The plan worked.

26

Washington assumed that after some recent wins the British commander would give his men a break to celebrate Christmas and their defenses would be down. In preparation, Washington had his men bring all the boats from the north side of the river where the British were encamped to the south side where his men would begin their crossing.

Despite being delayed, caught in a terrible blizzard, and undermanned, Washington's platoon of soldiers fought admirably and with heart. Their attitude and drive, along with Washington's creative surprise attack, lead to a huge defeat for the British, one that history has correctly viewed as a turning point in the American War of Independence.

Assess Your Skills: Creative Thinking

Take a moment to consider what you know about this concept and assess your skills. Indicate your level of agreement with each question.

How competent am I	Very little	Somewhat	Very much
Do I encourage my team to look for non-traditional solutions to problems?			
Do I make time for creative thinking?			
Am I able to synthesize diverse information, ideas, and recommendations into constructive solutions?			
Do I demonstrate an appreciation for creative thinking in the workplace?			
Is creativity rewarded in my organization?			

7 Tips – What To Do: Creative Thinking

The following tips will help you become more successful and continually improve your competence in this area. Check those that you need to develop.

☐ 1. Involve your work unit in problem solving and decision making and work as a team. Brainstorm ideas and make sure there is no judgment or criticism. Record every idea and take a break before evaluating ideas.

2. Provide employees (especially technical ones) with time for thinking, wondering, and experimenting. Demonstrate this yourself: Lead the way in thinking outside the box.

3. Encourage creative thinking. Explain that there is no one correct answer to a problem; it is okay to err, everyone can be creative, and no idea is foolish. Set up a suggestion system that allows for timely feedback and recognizes contributions. Implement good ideas.

4. List the problems facing you. Rewrite each problem as an objective. List several creative ways to reach each objective.

5. Observe how outside organizations are solving problems creatively. Adopt relevant ideas to fit your organization's needs.

6. Participate in professional organizations and stay current with professional literature to keep track of the newest developments in your field

7. Have department problem-solving discussions where the discussion flows spontaneously, all group members participate, and ideas are not evaluated until the end, when a decision must be reached.

Development Plan Resources: Creative Thinking

Build your expertise by reviewing the sources listed below:

Learning and Development Resources
Centrestar Academy. *Establishing an operational focus.* www.centrestar.com
Thomas, J. (2020). *Thinking differently: how to thrive using your nonlinear creative thinking.*
Trott, D. (2016). *One plus one equals three: a masterclass in creative thinking.*
Vogel, T. (2014). *Breakthrough thinking: A guide to creative thinking and idea generation.*

Remember this saying:
Necessity is the mother of invention.

26

Reflection and Application: Creative Thinking

Many organizations excel by encouraging their employees to be creative and allowing time for creative thinking. Google, for example, is famous for letting developers spend 20 percent of their paid work time on projects of their choice (Poh, n.d.). Some of Google's best ideas came from such programs (Poh, n.d.). Of course, not every organization needs or can afford this level of creativity, but creativity can be encouraged in every organization.

Leaders who foster creativity find ways to reward creativity (Poh, n.d.). Tasking teams with innovating in a specific area is also effective (Poh, n.d.). Perhaps the most important thing to remember whether you are engaging in creativity or encouraging creativity is that you must be willing to take risks.

Remember:

- Make time for creative thinking and reflection every day.
- Encourage creative thinking in your employees. Ensure they know creative thinking is allowed, encouraged – even expected – and that taking some calculated risks is acceptable.

The most important concept I learned about this competency is:

_____

_____

_____

To effectively apply this concept to my personal development I plan to:

_____

_____

_____

_____

_____

26

Creative thinking solves problems we did not yet know existed.

COMPETENCY 27
Vision

IMPORTANCE (I)	DEVELOPMENT NEED (DN)	VALUE (I x DN)
1 2 3 4 5	1 2 3 4 5	

Creates a shared vision of the organization; promotes wide ownership.

Leadership is the capacity to translate vision into reality.

– Warren Bennis[34]

Vision is two-fold. It is about having your own vision and the ability to see the big picture, but it is also about understanding and executing your organization's formal vision.

Leaders who excel carry-out their vision, making certain that their employees observe them as they live their vision. They also ensure that their vision is aligned with and supportive of the organization's vision. If the organization does not have a formal vision, these leaders help create one.

Leaders with vision not only understand the big picture, but also the individual projects within the organization. They see the end goal for each project, and also see how the various parts of the organization as well as the people need to come together to achieve every goal.

To clarify the concepts applicable to this competency, read the following list of observable and measurable knowledge, skills, tasks, and behaviors essential to all professionals:

- ✓ Creates a shared vision of the organization's future.

- ✓ Promotes wide ownership of the organization's vision.

- ✓ Understands and analyzes the broad perspective or big picture.

- ✓ Communicates and interprets the big picture to employees and others.

27

⭐🏃 *Leadership Learning:*
Vision

The Nature of Leadership

Owls have amazing physical vision that can inspire metaphorical vision in business leaders.

They say hindsight is 20/20 but the most effective leaders have tremendous foresight and vision. They use their visionary practices to promote broad ownership of their organizations. Visionary leaders are a unique group of individuals who see things as they should or could be, rather than how they are. They work to ensure that others come to share their vision and help bring it to fruition.

Nelson Mandela, John F. Kennedy, Rosa Parks, Martin Luther King Jr., Marie Curie, Steve Jobs, Gloria Steinem, Bill Gates, and Jeff Bezos are among some of the most notable visionaries of the modern era. These people achieved remarkable success in their own rights, and are indelibly unique; however, they all have exhibited the desire and drive to elicit change.

Much like owls that have binocular vision and can rotate their heads 270 degrees, these remarkable leaders discerned ways in which they could improve the world. Then, they looked forward, created a vision of how they wanted things to be, and brough their visions to life. In doing so, they left lasting, indelible marks on the world as we have come to know it.

As a result of their efforts: technology, equality, education, science, medicine, politics, policies, and lives have all been markedly improved. And with each new generation, new visions are brought to life and the ideals and innovations these extraordinary individuals conceived are improved upon. While we may never realize the ultimate impact of our discoveries, by creating, and sharing our visions with others we may start a ripple that will be evident long after our initial mark has been made.

Leading by Example: Vision

Real Life Leaders

Elon Musk looks beyond the present for the next extraordinary ideas at Tesla and SpaceX.

Elon Musk is known as a transformational leader, one with an eye toward new ideas, social change, and growth. He exhibits exceptional external awareness and vision , often looking beyond himself, beyond his company, and beyond the present for the next extraordinary idea. Musk is a dreamer, but also a doer.

As CEO of SpaceX and Tesla, Musk is purposeful and optimistic, as well as creative. He enjoys pushing boundaries by looking at the current state of affairs and then asking how he and his organizations can move forward to something bigger and better.

27

Take space, for example. Musk saw that all previous spacecraft were essentially disposable and that this disposability led to excessive costs that compromised future missions. Thus, Musk created SpaceX with a plan to create more reusable space machines, which he, in fact, did. While not without set-backs, SpaceX has reached heights of reusability that no other company – government or private – has yet achieved.

Musk does not push the envelope due to an excessive ego nor simply for the money. His purpose is to improve the human experience. Musk has taken on such lofty concepts as electric vehicles, global warming, and space travel because he wants, even needs, to help mankind push forward toward a better future. In so doing he demonstrates not only external awareness, but forward thinking as well.

Assess Your Skills: Vision

Take a moment to consider what you know about this concept and assess your skills. Indicate your level of agreement with each question.

How competent am I	Very little	Somewhat	Very much
Can I articulate the mission and vision of my organization?			
Am I aware of the internal strengths and weaknesses of my organization?			
Do I work with my team to create a shared vision of the organization's future?			
Am I well-read and knowledgeable about current issues in my field?			
Do I effectively share my visions for progress with my team members?			
Do I effectively communicate big picture issues to my employees?			

7 Tips – What To Do: Vision

27

The following tips will help you become more successful and continually improve your competence in this area. Check those that you need to develop.

☐ 1. Assess your organization's strengths, weaknesses, and opportunities, both internal and external, and create a vision for the future. Make certain that this vision is aligned with your organization's vision. Evaluate alternative routes and decide on the specific course to reach each desired outcome.

☐ 2. Participate in a planning session with colleagues to envision what the organization should be doing in the next three to five years. Prepare long-range and operational plans that are consistent with the organization's strategic planning goals.

☐ 3. Network with others on all levels of the organization to create and pursue the vision.

☐ 4. Read broadly to stay abreast of sociopolitical, economic, and technological trends that will affect the future direction of the organization in responding to society's needs.

☐ 5. Attend open management meetings to better understand the mission and strategic vision of the organization's leadership, and to understand when that vision changes.

☐ 6. Share the vision. Encourage buy-in by incorporating employee input and the strategic objectives that flow from the vision. Develop an organizational profile to determine your organization's performance capabilities based on existing and accessible resources and skills.

☐ 7. Volunteer to help a community-based organization formulate a vision and strategic plan.

Development Plan Resources: Vision

Build your expertise by reviewing the sources listed below:

Learning and Development Resources
Bennis, W. (2009). *On becoming a leader*. Perseus Publishing.
Centrestar Academy. *Developing leadership in organizations.* www.centrestar.com
Hagemann, B. (2017). *Leading with vision: the leader's blueprint for creating a compelling vision and engaging the workforce.*
Hyatt, M. (2020). *The vision-driven leader: 10 questions to focus your efforts, energize your team, and scale your business.*

27

"Where there is no vision, the people perish" – Proverbs 29:18 KJV

Reflection and Application: Vision

Leading with vision involves having a well-rounded perspective. You need to look at what is going on from various viewpoints, including those of stakeholders, employees, customers, partner organizations, suppliers, and contractors.

Remember:

- One part of having a vision involves networking with people at all levels of the organization to discuss the organizational vision.

- As a leader you must ensure that all employees understand and buy-in to the organization's mission and vision.

The most important concept I learned about this competency is:

_____

_____

_____

To effectively apply this concept to my personal development I plan to:

_____

_____

_____

_____

_____

_____

_____

_____

_____

27

Vision helps you see the forest and the trees.

COMPETENCY 28
External Awareness

IMPORTANCE (I)	DEVELOPMENT NEED (DN)	VALUE (I x DN)
1 2 3 4 5	1 2 3 4 5	

Stays informed on policies, priorities, trends and special interests and uses this information in making decisions; considers external impact of statements, decisions, and actions.

People are remarkably bad at remembering long lists of goals... Clarity comes with simplicity.

– Brendon Burchard[35]

Trying to lead an organization without having a firm awareness of influences external to the organization is like trying to navigate a maze in the dark. You can make guesses and feel your way, but you cannot make educated decisions nor be aware of the big picture.

Dynamic leadership requires an awareness of factors outside of the organization that may impinge upon what happens within the organization. Leaders must understand new and changing technologies, the technologies other companies are using, what laws and regulations impact the organization, as well as many additional factors.

Cutting-edge leaders also understand how an organization's statements and actions may affect external organizations and groups. In other words, effective leaders understand that no organization exists in a void.

To clarify the concepts applicable to this competency, read the following list of observable and measurable knowledge, skills, tasks, and behaviors essential to all professionals:

28

✓ Keeps up-to-date with laws, regulations, policies, procedures, trends, and developments that may affect areas of responsibility.

✓ Considers the external impact of statements or actions.

✓ Reviews and makes recommendations for revisions of policies, procedures, regulations, and laws affecting area of responsibility.

- ✓ Considers non-technical factors, such as political and socioeconomic developments, the media, and special interests in decision-making.

- ✓ Implements administrative priorities and initiatives in accomplishing organizational goals and activities.

Leadership Learning: External Awareness

The Nature of Leadership

Cats learn by observation and are aware and adaptable to their environment for survival.

There was once a little orange tabby cat roaming around outside, alone in the cruel harsh world. No one knew her story, perhaps she once had a warm home and a loving family. But now, she was lost outside wandering in the heat, rain, cold, and storms. She subsisted on bugs, rodents, and whatever else she could scavenge.

Practically skin and bones, she happened upon a house. The owners saw her and gave her some leftover turkey. Soon, she was living in their front yard. She enjoyed their petting, loved the food they provided, and she was relatively happy – she thought.

One day, the humans had grown so close to the cat that they brought her into their home. They cleaned her up, her food and water bowls of her own, and made her one of the family. Now, the cat knew true happiness.

One day the family tried to let the cat onto the front porch to enjoy the nice weather, but the cat wanted nothing of it. The cat looked out the window, safely behind glass.

28

Otherwise, friendly and calm the cat shook when thunder rumbled, hid when it rained, and would not venture anywhere near an open door. She had an external awareness of what the world was like out there and she did not want anything to do with it ever again.

As a leader in an organization, you cannot, like this cat, deny the reality of the world by staying behind glass. Instead, you must be aware of and take into account external events.

For some animals, being aware and adaptable has aided their survival. While bald eagles and cranes have struggled to thrive in human cities, pigeons have made the cities home. They build nests in structures, find food in the park, and know where they can safely go. Seagulls, too, have learned to accept their new reality. These birds are beach goers and boaters. They search trashcans for food, and beg picnickers for a bite, which includes sometimes swooping in and flying off with someone's sandwich. Like these animals, an aware leader is one who understands the dangers as well as the opportunities of the external world, and who knows how to maximize their organization's position within this environment.

Leading by Example: External Awareness

Real Life Leaders

28

Oprah Winfrey overcame the odds and empowered an entire generation of women to succeed.

There will always be those among us in leadership positions whose rise to success seems effortless, as though they have taken some sort of elevator that is largely inaccessible to others. Conversely, there are leaders who have struggled and overcome tremendous adversity to reach dazzling heights of success. Oprah Winfrey is the latter.

Ms. Winfrey, overcame abuse, numerous personal tragedies, and extreme poverty to become not only one of the greatest media moguls in history, but also one of the wealthiest women in the United States, and inarguably one of the most influential leaders of the twenty-first century, empowering generations of women to succeed. She has accomplished all this through education, not only in graduating college, but also going back in 1987 after leaving one credit shy of her degree to pursue her career in 1975, and also by staying informed on policies, priorities, trends, and special interests, and applying this information when making decisions.

Awareness and education are such vital components in her strategy for success that Ms. Winfrey's most famous quotes is "Education is the key to unlocking the world, a passport to freedom" (Winfrey, 2014). It is difficult to argue with this logic when it comes from a leader who has amassed a level of success few others have achieved.

Something else Ms. Winfrey learned early-on is the importance of considering the external impact of her statements, decisions, and actions. Choosing her words, and actions carefully has led to not only an unparalleled career, but also the respect of other leaders across the globe. Oprah Winfrey is the perfect example of overcoming the odds to achieve monumental success, and an inspiration to countless others in their pursuit of greatness.

Assess Your Skills: External Awareness

Take a moment to consider what you know about this concept and assess your skills. Indicate your level of agreement with each question.

How competent am I	Very little	Somewhat	Very much
Am I aware of the external opportunities and threats to my organization?			
Do I have a general awareness of our competition as far as technology, vision, and accomplishments?			
Am I aware of important laws and procedures in my organization and industry?			
Do I understand how the political, social, and economic climate impact my organization?			

28

Do I regularly read trade resources or attend seminars and trade-shows?			
Do I monitor customer trends and needs?			

7 Tips – What To Do: External Awareness

The following tips will help you become more successful and continually improve your competence in this area. Check those that you need to develop.

☐ 1. Join and actively participate in associations and professional organizations. Maintain professional contact with offices that help you stay up to date with policy, law, and regulation changes.

☐ 2. Attend trade shows. Vendors can be a wealth of knowledge about technology and competition.

☐ 3. Subscribe to and read journals in your area of expertise and in areas that you are not directly responsible for.

☐ 4. Study the demographic trends that could affect both the source of future labor and future markets for your organization's goods and services.

☐ 5. Evaluate the strategies of your competitors and understand how they operate in the marketplace. Have employees share specific trend information. Such a pooled resource establishes in-house expertise. Keep it up to date.

☐ 6. Make time to attend guest lectures or brown-bag lunches in your organization that are designed to inform employees of sociopolitical trends and developments in laws, policies, and regulations.

☐ 7. Stay abreast of federal policies by reading congressional newsletters and attending organizational meetings that update developments. Read daily and weekly news so that you are on top of political and social trends. Information is power.

28

Development Plan Resources: External Awareness

Build your expertise by reviewing the sources listed below:

Learning and Development Resources
Bensoussan, B.E. & Fleisher, C.S. (2015). *Analysis without paralysis: 12 tools to make better strategic decisions.*
Centrestar Academy. *Framing customer perceptions and expectations.* www.centrestar.com
Lippitt, M. (2019). *Situational mindsets: targeting what matters when it matters.*
Porter, M.E. (2008). *On competition, updated and expanded edition.*

Be mindful of the factors contributing to customer perceptions.

Reflection and Application: External Awareness

One way to develop external awareness is to network. Try attending trade shows, joining organizations, following websites, and using social media. Share information with your employees and other leaders.

Remember:
- You cannot lead without external awareness.
- External awareness involves understanding the industry, local demographics, customers, economics, and so forth.

28

The most important concept I learned about this competency is:

_____

_____

_____

_____

_____

_____

_____

_____

_____

_____

_____

_____

_____

_____

_____

_____

_____

_____

_____

_____

_____

_____

_____

28

To effectively apply this concept to my personal development I plan to:

_____

_____

_____

_____

_____

_____

_____

_____

_____

_____

_____

_____

_____

_____

_____

_____

_____

_____

_____

_____

_____

_____

28

_____

_____

_____

No organization exists in a vacuum.

COMPETENCY 29
Strategic Thinking and Planning

IMPORTANCE (I)	DEVELOPMENT NEED (DN)	VALUE (I x DN)
1 2 3 4 5	1 2 3 4 5	

Advocates and participates in strategic planning to define and achieve organizational goals.

Strategy without tactics is the slowest route to victory. Tactics without strategy is the noise before defeat.

— Sun Tzu[36]

A strategic thinker is a forward thinker, a person who surveys the situation, creates goals, and then develops steps to achieve those goals. You can apply strategic thinking and planning to short-term projects, and to long-term projects that move your organization forward. You might also use strategic thinking and planning in your personal life to prepare for events such as buying a house or retiring.

Strategic thinkers have both internal and external awareness, and they are capable of blending the two. SWOT (strengths, weaknesses, opportunities, threats) analyses are a productive way to do this. They give you an organized method for assessing the internal strengths and weaknesses of an organization, as well as the external opportunities and threats inherent within the organization and industry.

To clarify the concepts applicable to this competency, read the following list of observable and measurable knowledge, skills, tasks, and behaviors essential to all professionals:

- ✓ Thinks strategically as well as long term.

- ✓ Develops and adjusts strategic and other long-term plans.

- ✓ Develops and implements clearly defined goals and objectives based on the organization's mission and overall strategic plan.

- ✓ Adjusts strategic plans, goals, and objectives based on changes in environment, policy, customer feedback, and other new information.

29

Leadership Learning: Strategic Thinking and Planning

The Nature of Leadership

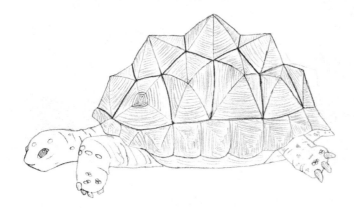

Tortoises use environmental landmarks and systematic strategies to efficiently find food in a radial maze.

As the female sea turtle swims through the open sea, she knows that when the instinct to reproduce arises she will return to the beach where she was born to lay her eggs. The same is true of the male; both return to the beach of their birth. Just offshore they will mate, then the female will crawl up the beach, dig a hole, and deposit her fertilized eggs. After covering the eggs with sand to hide them from predators the mother will return to the water, on her way again until the next breeding season.

Late at night following incubation, baby turtles push their way out of their eggs and start crawling toward the brightest light in the sky, which is the moon. With a little luck the fledgling turtles will make the trek without encountering predators. They will enter the sea and swim off to grow into adults. Later, they will make their own breeding journeys.

Sea turtles have a long-term goal. Hatch, follow the light to the water, eat, and survive, and then return to the beach to reproduce. For turtles you may call this instinct more than planning, but the result is the same – a set of planned actions (even if "coded" into their DNA) that increase the odds for success. Humans use strategic thinking and planning to achieve their long-term goals, as well.

29

Rather than thinking of yourself as a turtle following a preprogrammed path, imagine yourself as the creator who developed that plan for the turtles. Consider the forethought it took for God, nature, evolution – whatever you call it – to create this amazing plan and implement it. Build your own plan, think it through, and do it!

Leading by Example:
Strategic Thinking and Planning

Real Life Leaders

Mark Zuckerberg uses acquisition strategy to acquire tech services companies for Facebook.

Mark Zuckerberg, founder of the goliath Facebook, is a leader with vision, creativity, strategic thinking, and follow-through. We could discuss Zuckerberg's strategic thinking and planning in many ways, from his days in his dorm room brainstorming and creating the social media website Facebook, to his methods for so quickly growing the company to be worth billions.

Part of Zuckerberg's strategy has been to acquire up-and-coming tech service companies. Using Facebook's purchasing power, Zuckerberg beat-out rival Google, among others, to purchase companies such as Instagram, WhatsApp, and Oculus.

Zuckerberg's strategy has been to build relationships with the owners of companies and to present a shared vision, a clear plan for how the two companies can work together to accomplish a common goal (Heath, 2017). If that shared goal aligns with the company that he wants to acquire, the way is then opened.

While Zuckerberg prefers the strategies of getting to know a company's leaders and demonstrating a shared vision, he does not hesitate to use more authoritative methods when necessary to show smaller start-ups that it is difficult to thrive in the fast-paced tech world (Heath, 2017). He also knows how to move quickly to get the information he needs and put an offer on the table (Heath, 2017).

29

Assess Your Skills:
Strategic Thinking and Planning

Take a moment to consider what you know about this concept and assess your skills. Indicate your level of agreement with each question.

How competent am I	Very little	Somewhat	Very much
Am I a strategic, forward thinker?			
Do I create SMART (specific, measurable, achievable, relevant, time-bound) goals?			
Do I adjust my short-term goals to ensure that my long-term goals are on track?			
Do I respond to a changing external environment by adjusting goals or behaviors as necessary?			
Do I create goals for each working unit and communicate achievement of these goals?			

7 Tips – What To Do:
Strategic Thinking and Planning

The following tips will help you become more successful and continually improve your competence in this area. Check those that you need to develop.

1. Review the goals in your strategic plan to make sure that they are realistic and specific. Ask your colleagues and peers for feedback.

2. Review the mission, evaluate threats and opportunities in the environment, and plan specific actions each year. Be aware of any and all factors that can make an impact. Stay informed.

3. Examine the performance of best-in-class work units to understand what accounts for their success.

4. Develop strategic plans based on these questions: In what kind of business is this organization or department operating? What is its vision and mission?

5. Evaluate the strategic plans of other units to see how your unit compares, and to see what you can learn from others. Always be on top of market demographics.

29

6. Develop standards of work unit performance and communicate them to everyone involved. Be sure they get the latest information. Attend seminars and workshops to stay current with industry trends, changes, and standards.

7. Create a checklist to track how many deadlines are met in advance, on time, or missed, and build a project management system that will alert you to missed dates or deadlines.

Development Plan Resources: Strategic Thinking and Planning

Build your expertise by reviewing the sources listed below:

Learning and Development Resources
Centrestar Academy. *Facilitating strategic planning.* www.centrestar.com
Magretta, J. (2011). *Understanding Michael Porter: The essential guide to competition and strategy.*
McClean, D.R. (2020). *Strategic planning: As simple as A, B, C.*
OIson, A.K. & Simerson, B.K. (2015). *Leading with strategic thinking: Four ways effective leaders gain insight, drive change, and get results.*

According to USA Today Snapshots (Reilly and Tian, n.d.), MBA graduates – after one year in the workforce – wish they had received more education in strategic planning.

Reflection and Application: Strategic Thinking and Planning

While the phrase "thinking strategically" sounds like a promising activity, you will realize its value only through education and practical application. Strategic thinking and planning involve carrying out tasks with purpose and creating long-term goals. Strategic thinkers anticipate coming trends and look for exciting developments on the periphery of their industry (Shoemaker, 2012).

29

Remember:

- When you evaluate problems look for the root of the situation – the real cause – so that you can create a plan to solve the real issue (Shoemaker, 2012).
- Strategic thinking involves looking for patterns in data and asking good questions.
- Strategic thinkers use their interpersonal skills to see through people's agendas and uncover their motivations, which can help in strategic planning and negotiation (Shoemaker, 2012).

The most important concept I learned about this competency is:

_____

_____

_____

To effectively apply this concept to my personal development I plan to:

_____

_____

_____

_____

_____

_____

_____

_____

_____

_____

_____

29

_____

_____

Technology tools can assist you with strategic planning.

COMPETENCY 30
Management Controls

IMPORTANCE (I)	DEVELOPMENT NEED (DN)	VALUE (I x DN)
1 2 3 4 5	1 2 3 4 5	

Ensures the integrity of the organization's processes; promotes ethical and effective practices.

No business in the world has ever made money with poor management.

– Bill Terry[37]

Management controls involve various operational issues, but the focus is primarily on where the organization wants to be and how it plans to get there. For instance, an organization might review established employee performance standards or manufacturing standards, evaluate the difference between where the organization is and where it wants to be, and then develop strategic plans to bridge that gap.

Management controls imply ethical behavior. As a leader you are expected to foster a culture that promotes ethical conduct. This involves adopting ethical values, role modeling those values, and holding your employees accountable to standards.

To clarify the concepts applicable to this competency, read the following list of observable and measurable knowledge, skills, tasks, and behaviors essential to all professionals:

✓ Exercises necessary management controls to ensure the integrity of the organization's processes.

✓ Promotes and models ethical and effective practices in all organizational activities.

30

★ *Leadership Learning: Management Controls*

The Nature of Leadership

Dolphins are good at recognition and have been known to protect and rescue people from sharks.

Exercising management control involves behaving ethically, reacting responsibly and decisively, and doing what is right. Animals do this every day.

Off the coast of Italy, a 14-year-old boy and his father were spending the day on a boat. The father did not notice when his son fell overboard. As the boy sunk deeper into the water a well-known local dolphin named Filippo came to the boy's rescue, pushing him out of the water and close enough to the boat for the boy's father to pull the boy to safety ("Top 10", 2010). In another instance, in Monterey, California, a pod of dolphins protected a surfer from a shark by forming a ring around the shark-bitten surfer until he could ride a wave to shore ("Top 10", 2010).

At the Illinois Brookfield Zoo a toddler fell into a gorilla enclosure, hitting his head and losing consciousness. A female gorilla, with her own 17-month-old baby on her back, ran to protect the child from the other gorillas. She cradled the child in her arms, and then carried him 60 feet to the entrance where zoo-keepers retrieved him ("Top 10", 2010).

A woman was walking with her dog, Penny, along a riverbank. The woman noticed an empty wheelchair on the water's edge, and then, looking out over the water, she saw a body floating. The woman ordered her dog to "Fetch!" while pointing to the body. Penny leapt into the water and pulled the floating woman to shore ("Top 10", 2010).

When managers understand the value of exercising ethical and responsible control, they are better poised to make good decisions. As always, actions speak louder than words.

Leading by Example:
Management Controls

Real Life Leaders

Alan Mulally is known for listening, planning, managing, and accomplishing goals at Ford.

Alan Mulally, retired CEO of Ford Motor Company, has a reputation for excellent management controls and strategy. In fact, his leadership style and planning strategies are so effective that he is emulated and revered by many industries, including healthcare.

Mulally's leadership philosophy included (Rappleye, 2015) the following ideas:

- **Flatten the organization with an open door and spirit of comradery**

    Mulally interacted with employees. For example, he ate with them in the cafeteria, talked to them about their concerns and ideas, emailed them for input, and so on. This helped him understand the needs and insights of his employees.

30

- **Help employees work together**

  Mulally eliminated rank to encourage cooperation as opposed to competition. He also fostered a team-based environment that was respectful and appreciative.

- **Consolidate and specialize**

  Mulally sold off certain profitable areas of the company to allow Ford to focus on its key mission and customer needs.

- **Data driven listening**

  Mulally accessed the organization's data and then listened to management staff, gathering their impressions, understanding of the data, and points of view.

As CEO of Ford, Mulally was a man who led by listening and planning, and who managed by keeping his eye on the goal and striving steadily toward accomplishing that goal, ethically and responsibly.

 Assess Your Skills: Management Controls

Take a moment to consider what you know about this concept and assess your skills. Indicate your level of agreement with each question.

How competent am I	Very little	Somewhat	Very much
Am I good at controlling organizational processes?			
Do I stress conformance to financial integrity standards?			
Through my behavior, do I exhibit my commitment to ethical behavior?			
Do I act decisively to deal with ethical breaches in the organization?			
Do I avoid even the appearance of impropriety?			

7 Tips – What To Do:
Management Controls

The following tips will help you become more successful and continually improve your competence in this area. Check those that you need to develop.

☐ 1. Act as a role model by conforming to organizational and financial integrity standards.

☐ 2. React decisively to instances of ethical or financial impropriety among employees, vendors, contractors, or grantees. Be certain that your employees make appropriate decisions when they face "gray area" ethical choices.

☐ 3. Develop a process flowchart for a major activity within your area of responsibility and identify and evaluate the major control points. Track and monitor change indicators and act accordingly.

☐ 4. Identify the objectives and control techniques appropriate for your area of operational responsibility.

☐ 5. Familiarize yourself with the organization's code of ethical behavior; exhibit and encourage ethical behavior beyond what is required by law.

☐ 6. Err on the conservative side if there is a question about the ethical integrity of a decision or action. Never make decisions when in doubt about ethics. Instead, rely on mentors and your legal department.

☐ 7. Establish as a strategic priority the elimination of all non-value-added tasks in your work organization; challenge the status quo in order to make this happen.

30

Development Plan Resources: Management Controls

Build your expertise by reviewing the sources listed below:

Learning and Development Resources
Centrestar Academy. *Understanding project budgeting and justification.* www.centrestar.com
Delaney, D. (2013). *New business networking: How to effectively grow your business networks using on-line and off-line methods.*
Doerr, J. (2018). *Measure what matters: How Google, Bono, and The Gates Foundation rock the world with OKRs.*
Donahue, W. (2021). *Unlocking Lean Six Sigma.*

Everything in business is bound by money. Even the most extraordinary project must adhere to a budget, must strive to be cost-effective, and must justify expenses.

Reflection and Application: Management Controls

When it comes to management controls it is important to role model ethical and responsible behavior. Believe in and live your organizational values.

Remember:

- Always err on the side of caution when ethics are in question; this means avoiding even the appearance of impropriety.
- Work toward continual improvement, which is an important part of management controls.
- Encourage employees to discuss "gray area" ethical choices with their managers.

The most important concept I learned about this competency is:

30

To effectively apply this concept to my personal development I plan to:

_____

_____

_____

_____

_____

_____

_____

_____

_____

_____

_____

_____

_____

_____

_____

_____

_____

_____

_____

_____

30

Ethics and responsibility are essential aspects of leadership behavior.

Competency 31
Diverse Workforce

IMPORTANCE (I)	DEVELOPMENT NEED (DN)	VALUE (I x DN)
1 2 3 4 5	1 2 3 4 5	

Recognizes the value of cultural, ethnic, gender, and other individual difference; provides employment and development opportunities for a diverse workforce.

An individual hasn't started living until he can rise above the narrow confines of his individualistic concerns to the broader concerns of all humanity.

– Martin Luther King, Jr.[38]

"Cultural diversity is important because our country, workplaces, and schools increasingly consist of various cultural, racial, and ethnic groups. We can learn from one another, but first we must have a level of understanding about each other to facilitate collaboration and cooperation." (Belfield, 2018).

When people come together, they bring their individual experiences, expectations, strengths, and weaknesses. This can lead to a new level of creativity, development, and understanding for all concerned. While valuing diversity is critical for success, you must also be prepared to handle issues that a diverse workforce or customer base can bring.

To clarify the concepts applicable to this competency, read the following list of observable and measurable knowledge, skills, tasks, and behaviors essential to all professionals:

✓ Recognizes the value of cultural, ethnic, gender, and other individual differences at all levels of the organization.

✓ Promotes inclusivity.

✓ Provides employment and development opportunities for a diverse workforce.

✓ Increases the sensitivity of others to diversity issues through formal and informal means.

31

Leadership Learning:
Diverse Workforce

The Nature of Leadership

Ocean inhabitants – are an example of the diversity of creatures and natural process.

Today, *diversity* is a buzzword in business, politics, and society. But diversity, and the value of diversity, is not a new concept. It is diversity that has always made nature so beautiful and awe-inspiring. Consider the allure of diversified landscapes, plants, and animals. Diversity enhances the world.

For example, bees land on flowers, picking up nectar and pollen. As they move to the next plant, they inadvertently deposit some of the pollen as they pick up new nectar. Then, they use that nectar to make honey, which is eaten by creatures as diverse as bears and humans. The deposit of pollen from diverse buds also enables plants to produce new plants. The world is beautiful – and tasty place – due to the variety of creatures, plants, and processes it inspires.

As an example, ocean water is kept clean due to the diverse needs of diverse creatures. Some eat plankton, while others eat algae, and so help to clean these environments. Imagine how dirty the seas and lakes would be if there were no catfish and other bottom-dwelling scavengers.

31

Consider the diversity of creatures and natural processes which take part in maintaining a working ecosphere. On land, squirrels and rodents scavenge for seeds and bugs, which helps to keep insect populations in check and limits the spread of plants and trees. Bears eat berries and seeds. Giraffes, rather than competing for food on the savanna floor, eat from high in the trees. Vultures help keep areas free of rotting carcasses.

In the human world, diversity is equally significant. When people of different backgrounds, with diverse experiences and various demographics come together, each has an opportunity to see things from new perspectives and to work together to accomplish more than any single individual or group could do alone.

Leading by Example: Diverse Workforce

Real Life Leaders

Julie Sweet drove her organization, Accenture, to be recognized by Forbes as one of the best workplaces places for diversity.

Few things more ardently stoke the fires of innovation than diversity. The greater the range of unique individuals in a conglomerate, the greater the opportunity for distinctive ideals. Cultivating a diverse workforce that recognizes the value of cultural, ethnic, gender, and other individual differences is perhaps one of the greatest strategies an organization can employ.

Julie Sweet, CEO of Accenture, has effectively put this tactic into practice, as is evident by the company's recognition by Forbes as one of the best workplaces for diversity. One of the ways Sweet has made strides to provide employment and development opportunities for a diverse workforce is by implementing a new purpose for the organization, seeking to "deliver on the promise of technology and human ingenuity" (Karlgaard, 2020).

31

Creating a diverse workplace is not only the socially responsible thing to do but it is also one of the most beneficial things an organization can do to increase their bottom line (Page, 2019). Employing individuals from varying political, ethnic,

religious, economic, educational, and assorted other backgrounds helps ensure a company is receiving ideas, feedback, and solutions from many points of view.

It is easy to become overwhelmed in the workplace, especially when we are not seeing the results we desire. Albert Einstein once said, "The definition of insanity is doing the same thing over and over again, but expecting different results." By this logic, employing individuals who offer unique perspectives and insights, and harkening to their suggestions guarantees different outcomes.

Assess Your Skills: Diverse Workforce

Take a moment to consider what you know about this concept and assess your own skills. Indicate your level of agreement with each question.

How competent am I	Very little	Somewhat	Very much
Do I understand the benefits of diversity?			
Am I familiar with the laws regarding diversity in the workplace?			
Do I show a commitment to diversity in my organization?			
Through my behavior, do I encourage team members to treat each other with respect?			
Am I sensitive to the issues of diverse employee groups?			
Does my understanding of diversity help me be a better leader?			
Does my organization hold diversity training sessions?			
Does my understanding of diversity help me meet the needs of our customers?			

31

7 Tips – What To Do: Diverse Workforce

The following tips will help you become more successful and continually improve your competence in this area. Check those that you need to develop.

☐ 1. Hold diversity workshops for employees and always act promptly to intolerance.

☐ 2. Have a discussion with your colleagues about the effects of discrimination. Ask them if it exists within the organization. If so, ask for ideas on how to eliminate it.

☐ 3. Examine the demographic, ethnic, and cultural profile of your work unit to see whether it reflects diversity. If it does not, examine causes and strategies for correcting the situation.

☐ 4. Familiarize yourself with the organization's Affirmative Action and EEO rules and policies.

☐ 5. Consider developmental assignments for members of protected groups. Focus on supporting career development for all members of your team, department, or organization.

☐ 6. Enjoy the diversity of dispositions and capabilities in your work unit. Capitalize on the diversity by devising ways to draw individuals with unique talents into the work process.

☐ 7. Consider having all members of your work unit take an interpersonal styles inventory so everyone understands and develops a healthy' respect for style differences within the group.

31

Development Plan Resources:
Diverse Workforce

Build your expertise by reviewing the sources listed below:

Learning and Development Resources
Aguilar, E. (2020). *Coaching for equity: Conversations that change practice.*
Centrestar Academy. *Communicating respectfully in today's workplace.* www.centrestar.com
Espinoza, C. & Ukleja, M. (2016).). *Managing the millennials: discover the core competencies for managing today's workforce.*
Fuller, P. (2020). *The leader's guide to unconscious bias.*

For the first time in U.S. history there are five generations employed in the workplace.

Reflection and Application:
Diverse Workforce

Diversity is the future and must be valued in the workplace. A leader must understand the law surrounding protected groups and require employees to do the same.

Remember:

- Strive to have a diverse workforce and embrace it, partly because your workforce should reflect your customer base to some extent (Feigenbaum, 2015).

- Hiring employees from various cultural backgrounds and who speak different languages can help you reach new customers (Feigenbaum, 2015).

- Not only must you ethically and realistically embrace diversity and value it, but you must learn to work well with diverse people and encourage cooperation.

31

The most important concept I learned about this competency is:

31

To effectively apply this concept to my personal development I plan to:

_____

_____

_____

_____

_____

_____

_____

_____

_____

_____

_____

_____

_____

_____

_____

_____

_____

_____

_____

_____

_____

_____

_____

31

The business environment becomes more diverse every day. Embracing the diversity of your employees, suppliers, and customers is imperative.

COMPETENCY 32
Leading Change

IMPORTANCE (I)	DEVELOPMENT NEED (DN)	VALUE (I x DN)
1 2 3 4 5	1 2 3 4 5	

Leads organizational transformation and change efforts; champions organizational change.

Change is the law of life. And those who look only to the past or present are certain to miss the future.

– John F. Kennedy[39]

Change is inevitable. A true leader does not fear change, does not avoid change, but rather embraces it and looks for ways to implement it positively. At no time in the history of business does change occur more rapidly than it does today. It is imperative that you embrace change and adapt to it.

A forward-looking leader is proactive, constantly watching the horizon for change, anticipating it, and staying a step ahead of it. Sometimes, change appears to be positive, like the introduction of a technology that will make life easier. Other times, it seems to have a positive potential, but the process of change still seems foreboding. Still, other times, change clearly seems unpleasant, yet it cannot be stopped. In all these situations, a proactive leader must model a positive attitude towards change and help the workplace adapt to it as painlessly as possible.

To clarify the concepts applicable to this competency, read the following list of observable and measurable knowledge, skills, tasks, and behaviors essential to all professionals:

- ✓ Initiates and facilitates cultural and technological change in the organization; acts as a change agent.

- ✓ Respects and adapts to change.

- ✓ Creates an environment that empowers and supports others in a change process or changing organization.

32

Leadership Learning:
Leading Change

The Nature of Leadership

Bar-tailed godwit can fly nearly 700 miles without stopping while embracing a change of environment.

Change is not easy. Take the bar-tailed godwit, a small seabird that migrates from Alaska to New Zealand every year. These long-beaked, white and brown, long-legged wading birds are born in Alaska, but once they reach four months old, the fledglings join a flock of 10 to more than 100 birds to make an epic flight across the Pacific to New Zealand. There, the birds spend their first few years, until they themselves are ready to breed, at which time they make the epic journey back to Alaska.

Birds of breading age make the flight every year, leaving Alaska in the fall and flying nearly 700 miles to New Zealand, without stopping. Flying at a speed of 35 miles per hour, this little bird flaps and flies for eight or nine days straight – a record breaker among both birds and airplanes. In the spring, they return to Alaska to breed, and then head back to New Zealand again in the fall, in a never ending cycle.

While the bar-tailed godwit is not alone in embracing change through migration, it is among the most remarkable. Human supervisors, too, need to embrace change and in fact, need to lead change, championing change in a way that helps employees accept, understand, and embrace change.

32

Leading by Example:
Leading Change

Real Life Leaders

Elizabeth Cady Stanton is known for her tireless fighting for female voting rights and American social reform.

Change is inevitable, and truly effective leaders step-up, take charge and champion organizational transformation and change efforts. One such pioneering leader was Elizabeth Cady Stanton. Though often overshadowed by her dear friend and counterpart in the women's liberation movement, Susan B. Anthony, Stanton worked tirelessly to further the progress of women's rights in the United States. Alongside Anthony, she fought zealously for female voting rights and American social reform.

Stanton understood then in the mid-1800s what many scholars are only now coming to discover, and is the value of emotional intelligence in effecting change. This knowledge is particularly significant when one considers the fact that Stanton was an undeniably effective trailblazer during a time when women were largely seen as too emotional to be efficacious leaders.

Overcoming challenges to implement changes is a hallmark of stellar leadership and emotional intelligence plays a significant role in those efforts (Issah, 2018). By working in conjunction with Anthony, Stanton determined the most effective verbiage for their literature and speeches, and she produced some of the most influential propaganda of her time. Her work resulted in organizational transformation and change efforts that are still prevalent today, over 100 years later.

32

In addition to understanding and using emotional intelligence, Stanton knew the importance of aligning oneself with like-minded individuals and playing to each person's individual strength to help facilitate common efforts. While Anthony was well known as the orator of the duo, it was Stanton who did the majority of the writing. Had only one of these remarkable ladies sought to bring about changes and reform they would not have been nearly so effective.

Assess Your Skills:
Leading Change

Take a moment to consider what you know about this concept and assess your skills. Indicate your level of agreement with each question.

How competent am I	Very little	Somewhat	Very much
Am I open to change in my workplace and industry?			
Do I stay abreast of changes in my industry, technology, and customer base?			
Do I adapt easily to change and with a positive attitude?			
Do I champion change in the workplace?			
Do I recognize how difficult change can be for my team?			
Do I help employees work through times of change?			
Do I proactively look for situations where change is needed?			

7 Tips – What To Do:
Leading Change

The following tips will help you become more successful and continually improve your competence in this area. Check those that you need to develop.

☐ 1. List all the problems facing you. Rewrite each problem as an objective. List several creative ways to reach each objective.

2. Involve your work unit in making decisions about trying and refining new ideas.

3. Survey colleagues to determine where change might be needed in your area.

4. Before any change is put into place, meet with stakeholders to explain the change and how it will affect them. Involve people in the planning and design of the change.

5. Participate in professional organizations and stay current with the professional literature regarding new developments in your field.

6. Provide colleagues (especially technical ones) with time for thinking, wondering, and experimenting. Across the board, consider solving problems through team brainstorming.

7. Encourage colleagues to continually update their skills by supporting their training and development plans, sharing information with them on external trends, and showing enthusiasm for their creative ideas. Set up a suggestion system that responds to and recognizes contributions.

Development Plan Resources: Leading Change

Build your expertise by reviewing the sources listed below:

Learning and Development Resources
Bridges, W. (2017). *Managing transitions: making the most of change.*
Centrestar Academy. *Implementing Organizational Change Initiative.* www.centrestar.com
Health, C. & Heath, D. (2020). *Switch: How to change things when change is hard.*
Kotter, J.P. (2012). *Leading change.*

We are living a technological revolution. You may not always have all the facts, nonetheless, a leader's job is to create a climate open to and supportive of change.

Reflection and Application: Leading Change

32

Even positive change is rarely easy; unwanted change can seem an insurmountable task. But, with planning, a positive attitude, and communication, any organization will not only survive change, but will thrive as a result.

Remember:

- Be an agent of change. Look for disruptive innovation or ways that you can be a leader in your industry.
- Champion change in your workplace by role modeling a positive attitude and displaying confidence.

The most important concept I learned about this competency is:

_____

_____

_____

To effectively apply this concept to my personal development I plan to:

_____

_____

_____

_____

_____

_____

_____

_____

_____

_____

_____

_____

32

The best way to survive change is to lead change.

Competency Cluster E:
Technical Acumen

The nation behaves well if it treats the natural resources as assets which it must turn over to the next generation increased, and not impaired, in value.

– Theodore Roosevelt[40]

New technologies, and our use of technology, are growing at a phenomenal pace. From engineering to medicine, fast food to plumbing, no part of our world is free from technology. Smart phones, computers, and electronic gadgets are suddenly global necessities.

Today, as an employee and as a leader, you must not only know how to use these technologies to be successful in the workplace, but you must also know how to use them to competitive advantage.

Here we describe three competencies revolving around **job-specific technical skills**, **occupational technical skills**, and **industry-wide technical skills** of concern to all leaders.

COMPETENCY 33
Job-Specific Technical Competencies

IMPORTANCE (I)	DEVELOPMENT NEED (DN)	VALUE (I x DN)
1 2 3 4 5	1 2 3 4 5	

Demonstrates knowledge, skills, and abilities and uses proper methods and procedures to successfully carry out job responsibilities within an organization or work group.

I'm a great believer in luck, and I find the harder I work, the more I have of it.

– Thomas Jefferson[41]

As you study this competency consider what your technical skills were when you began your job and how those skills have evolved over time. We are certain these skills have gone through tremendous growth. Consider the following questions: How did you expand your skills? What you do well? What can you improve on now?

With regard to technology, consider what requirements, regulations, laws, and organizational policies affect your job. Make sure that you understand the role you play in your organization, and that you constantly work to keep your technological job skills current.

To clarify the concepts applicable to this competency, read the following list of observable and measurable knowledge, skills, tasks, and behaviors essential to all professionals:

✓ Demonstrates job-specific technical proficiency in areas of responsibility.

✓ Understands and considers the job-specific technical difficulties and complexities placed on others by the nature of their work.

✓ Appropriately applies job-specific technological procedures, requirements, regulations, and policies related to area of expertise.

33

Leadership Learning: Job-Specific Technical Competencies

The Nature of Leadership

Vultures have specific skills that get the job done and help keep the environment free of decaying flesh and thus disease.

Every job has a specific skillset necessary to get the job done. Some are more complicated than others, and some may be more enjoyable than others, but there are always some skills that you must demonstrate to be judged as proficient in your job.

The common vulture is as an example of specific skills that may not seem enjoyable but that do get the job done. Not a particularly attractive bird, and sometimes the brunt of negative comments, this bird has a crucial job to do, one for which it is well suited.

Vultures almost never attack healthy prey; in fact, they most often feast on dead animals. In this way, they help keep environments free of decaying flesh and thus disease.

Vultures feed themselves by gorging when food is available and storing the food in a compartment that is part of the digestive system called the crop until it can be digested. Vultures have strong stomach acids, which allows them to eat dead, decaying, and even infected flesh without becoming sick. Vultures play an important part in keeping the earth clean. Without them a large variety of deadly bacteria would spread easily.

Another beneficial process carried out by the vulture is urination. When vultures release liquid waste it runs straight down their legs. The uric acid in the waste helps

33

to kill germs that vultures pick up on their legs by walking over carcasses, and it also aids in regulating body temperature.

Understanding, and embracing, the specific skills necessary to do your job is essential to your success. You must also have at least a working understanding of the skills necessary for your employees to perform their jobs.

Leading by Example: Job-Specific Technical Competencies

Real Life Leaders

Tim Cook kept Apple true to its culture, mission, and technical competencies.

Let us compare apples to apples for a minute and talk about the technical acumen and leadership ability of Tim Cook, the man who recently followed in Jobs' footsteps as CEO of Apple. Cook understands the Apple organization that Jobs created. Cook knows that innovating new features to meet customer expectations is at the core (no pun intended) of what people expect.

When Cook first took over, he realized that people would fear change, and Cook recognized that part of his job was to allay those fears. He did this immediately via a memo that acknowledged the legacy of Apple culture and what he called Apple's DNA. Cook knew his job: To empower. Encourage. Embolden. And move forward.

Yet, Cook did not try to be Jobs. Cook is his own man. Hi is more reserved, disdaining the spotlight, yet still leading the way. Tim Cook has kept Apple at the top of the technological hierarchy by promoting diversity and innovation, by staying true

33

to Apple's culture and mission, and by understanding his own role in the company and, by doing his job skillfully and effectively.

Assess Your Skills:
Job-Specific Technical Competencies

Take a moment to consider what you know about this concept and assess your skills. Indicate your level of agreement with each question.

How competent am I	Very little	Somewhat	Very much
Do I have the technical skills necessary to do my own job well?			
Have I ensured that someone else has the technical competence to do my job should unexpected circumstances make me unavailable?			
Do I know what laws, regulations, and policies impact my area of technical expertise?			
Am I aware of technological advances in my specific area of work?			
Am I well-rounded, having technical skills in a variety of areas within my organization?			
Do I keep my technical skills current?			
Do I know where to go if I have technical questions?			

7 Tips – What To Do:
Job-Specific Technical Competencies

The following tips will help you become more successful and continually improve your competence in this area. Check those that you need to develop.

☐ 1. Network with other professionals in your industry. Keep a list of relevant technological resources in the industry.

☐ 2. Be aware of technological advances that could impact your industry.

33

3. Keep a log of the technical questions and industry-related problems for which others ask your assistance. Analyze how you helped them to determine their technological strengths and weaknesses.

4. Find others in your organization who are strong in the technological skills or knowledge of your industry that you are weak in. Ask to observe, work with, and get feedback from them.

5. Try to become the industry expert in your organization in one or more technical areas. Make yourself available as a sounding board for technical ideas.

6. Continually update your knowledge of technology, policies, and regulations that apply to your area of expertise and ensure that all projects accommodate the requirements.

7. Maintain proficiency in your technical area of expertise by remaining involved in your industry and by keeping current with technical literature and developments. When making technical judgments, use pools of available talent to support your ideas.

Development Plan Resources: Job-Specific Technical Competencies

Build your expertise by reviewing the sources listed below:

Learning and Development Resources
Centrestar Academy. *Lean-Sigma Process Improvement Yellow Belt.* www.centrestar.com
Donahue, W. (2021). *Unlocking Lean Six Sigma.*
Pearse, M. & Dunwoody, M. (2013). *Learning that never ends: Qualities of a lifelong learner.*
Rothwell, W., Donahue, W., Park, J. (2001). *Creating In-House Sales Training and Development Programs*

Leaders must understand job-specific technical competencies and how to identify areas where improvement is needed and apply skills.

33

Reflection and Application: Job-Specific Technical Competencies

One important concept in evaluating your job-specific technical competencies is to maintain your proficiency in those skills but also to be willing to consult with others when you have questions or concerns.

Remember:

- Regularly evaluate your employees to determine how current their job-specific technical competencies are.

- As a leader, you may not have a technical responsibility in your workplace; however, it is to your advantage to find at least one area in the organization where you are the technical authority and go-to person.

The most important concept I learned about this competency is:

_____

_____

_____

To effectively apply this concept to my personal development I plan to:

_____

_____

_____

_____

_____

_____

_____

_____

_____

Before you can lead you must know your own job.

33

COMPETENCY 34
Occupational Technical Competencies

IMPORTANCE (I)	DEVELOPMENT NEED (DN)	VALUE (I x DN)
1 2 3 4 5	1 2 3 4 5	

Demonstrates knowledge, skills, and abilities needed within current occupation (such as engineer, HR professional, lawyer, nurse) and stays current with the changes and developments in the occupation.

The technical is not just the machinery. The technical is a disposition to life.

– Leon Kass[42]

Occupational technical competence involves the ability to understand and apply all the technical competencies required in your occupation. For example, imagine you are a supervisor at a printing company. One job-specific competency might be the ability to operate a printing press. But occupational technical competencies might also include understanding how to clean, load, and even conduct minor repairs on the printing press.

Some experts assert that occupational technical competency involves three aspects (CV Tech, n.d.): knowledge of how to accomplish a task, skill in accomplishing a task, and the necessary attitude to be productive in a task (CV Tech, n.d.).

To clarify the concepts applicable to this competency, read the following list of observable and measurable knowledge, skills, tasks, and behaviors essential to all professionals:

✓ Demonstrates technical proficiency and currency in areas of occupational responsibility.

✓ Understands and considers the technical difficulties and complexities placed upon others by the nature of their occupational work.

✓ Appropriately applies procedures, requirements, regulations, and policies related to specialized occupational area of expertise.

34

Leadership Learning:
Occupational Technical Competencies

The Nature of Leadership

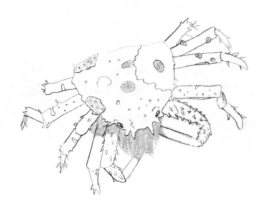

Decorator crab have developed a unique job for themselves as trash collectors with a purpose.

The decorator crab is a small marine crab with an interesting way of carrying out the job of living. Crabs are tasty treats for a variety of sea creatures, so they must protect themselves. The decorator crab solved its protection problem by creating a unique job: It is a trash collector with a purpose.

The decorator crab collects debris from the ocean floor and attaches the debris to its shell. This allows the crab to blend in better with its environment as well as to take cover. In the wild the decorator crab will pick up shells, dead coral, bits of sponge, and even living anemones, and attach them to the top of its shell. It covers so much of its shell that it becomes almost unrecognizable as a crab. When it seeks to hide from a predator or sneak up on a food source, the crab will sit down and hide beneath its elaborate protective gear. In captivity, a decorator crab will attach anything available to its shell, including aquarium ornaments, plastic cups, and so on.

In short, the decorator crab adapts, drawing on the resources in its surroundings for protection and camouflage. Similarly, employees must draw on the talents of others, help others to achieve their own competence, and take part in making the workplace technically capable of accomplishing each job.

Leading by Example: Occupational Technical Competencies

Real Life Leaders

Howard Schultz was known as a forward thinker at Starbucks who understood the industry and the practical use of technology by customers.

Many of us know the saying "Jack of all trades, master of none" but not everyone realizes that this is not the entire quote. The full quote is "Jack of all trades, master of none, but often times better than a master of one."

The most effective leaders understand they cannot afford to be simply a "master of one". To be truly effective, a leader must develop and master multiple occupational technical competencies. They must: demonstrates knowledge, skills, and abilities needed within current occupation (such as engineer, HR professional, lawyer, nurse) and stay current with relevant occupational changes and developments.

One such individual is the former CEO of Starbucks, Howard Schultz. Schultz is highly regarded as a true visionary who understands industry in general as well as the important role technology plays in business, particularly where customers are concerned. From the intricate machines from which their world-famous beverages are made, to their intuitive phone app, their partnerships with music streaming service Spotify, and software giant Microsoft, Starbucks is continually seeking to implement new technology whenever possible in an effort to not only streamline their work, but also reduce their carbon footprint, and at the same time make the "Starbucks experience" more pleasant for their customers.

34

Leaders can never master everything. But they must continually seek to garner new knowledge and remain "on top of" new developments in their field. For instance, we would not be apt to seek the advice of a physician who graduated in 1980 but has not pursued any further education since. That is why each state's medical board has requirements for continuing education to maintain one's license to practice medicine.

Assess Your Skills: Occupational Technical Competencies

Take a moment to consider what you know about this concept and assess your skills. Indicate your level of agreement with each question.

How competent am I	Very little	Somewhat	Very much
Do I understand the technology my team or organization uses and ensure that it is appropriate?			
Do my employees have a backup that has the necessary skill in case of prolonged absenteeism?			
Do I apply and enforce procedures, regulations, and policies in the workplace?			
Do I stay current with the kinds of technology used in my workplace?			
Do I understand the level of technical skill my employees must have?			
Do I regularly evaluate the skills and technical expertise of my team?			

7 Tips – What To Do: Occupational Technical Competencies

The following tips will help you become more successful and continually improve your competence in this area. Check those that you need to develop.

☐ 1. Network with fellow occupational professionals; list relevant resources.

☐ 2. Technological advances can impact your industry overnight. Stay informed!

34

☐ 3. Keep a log of the technical questions and industry problems for which others ask your assistance. Analyze how you were able to help them to better determine your strengths and weaknesses.

☐ 4. Seek out experts in your industry, those who have more advanced skills or knowledge. Ask to observe, work with, and get feedback from them.

☐ 5. Try to become the industry expert in your organization in one or more technical areas. Make yourself available as a sounding board for technical ideas.

☐ 6. Continually update your technological, policy, and regulation knowledge that applies to your occupational area of expertise, so all projects can meet requirements.

☐ 7. Maintain proficiency in your occupational area of expertise by remaining involved in your profession: Read technical literature and learn about advances in your industry. When making technical judgments, use pools of available talent to support these ideas.

Development Plan Resources: Occupational Technical Competencies

Build your expertise by reviewing the sources listed below:

Learning and Development Resources
Centrestar Academy. *Leading for Corporate Innovation.* www.centrestar.com
Costa, A.L. & Kallick, B. (2009). *Learning and leading habits of the mind: 16 essential characteristics for success.*
Horowitz, B. (2019). *What you do is who you are: How to create your business culture.*
Yeh, C. (2018). *Blitzscaling: The lightning-fast path to building massively valuable companies.*

Customers today look for organizations and contractors that are ethical, honest, impeccable in their word, and technically competent.

34

Reflection and Application: Occupational Technical Competencies

Being a leader involves working with your employees to determine whether they have the technical and occupational competencies they need to do their jobs, and to help the entire organization succeed.

Remember:

- Make certain that you are technically competent to serve as an occupational resource to others in your organization.
- Create networks in your organization through which people can gain technical support and share information.

The most important concept I learned about this competency is:

_____

_____

_____

To effectively apply this concept to my personal development I plan to:

_____

_____

_____

_____

_____

_____

_____

_____

_____

A leader must understand all the technical roles in the organization.

34

COMPETENCY 35
Industry-Wide Technical Competencies

IMPORTANCE (I)	DEVELOPMENT NEED (DN)	VALUE (I x DN)
1 2 3 4 5	1 2 3 4 5	

Demonstrates knowledge, skills, and abilities needed within an industry (such as manufacturing, hospitality, financial services, education, healthcare, transportation) and stays current with changes and developments in the industry.

You never change things by fighting the existing reality. To change something, build a new model that makes the existing model obsolete. America should lead on science and technology and Americans should win the race on the kinds of discoveries that unleash new jobs.

– R. Buckminster Fuller[43]

In addition to job-specific competencies, as a leader you must have, or have at least an understanding of the technical competencies within your entire industry. Returning to our printing example, the printer must know at least a bit about every area of the printing company including how to do layout, copy editing, product design, printing, folding, packaging, marketing – everything involved in the process.

To clarify the concepts applicable to this competency, read the following list of observable and measurable knowledge, skills, tasks, and behaviors essential to all professionals:

✓ Demonstrates technical proficiency in industry competencies and area of expertise.

✓ Understands and considers the technical difficulties and complexities placed upon employees by the nature of their work in the industry.

✓ Appropriately applies procedures, requirements, regulations, and policies related to the industry and area of expertise.

35

Leadership Learning: Industry-Wide Technical Competencies

The Nature of Leadership

Raccoons have impeccable memories, hearing, and technical skills, and can even pick locks.

Both occupational technical competencies and industry-wide technical competencies require a continual investment in education to stay current with relevant industry changes and developments. Business leaders within any trade must also demonstrate knowledge, skills, and abilities needed within their particular industry (such as manufacturing, hospitality, financial services, education, healthcare, transportation).

Some of the greatest attributes an industry leader can possess are: knowledge; trustworthiness; objectivity; fair-mindedness; excellent memories; exemplary listening and communication skills; a proclivity for innovation; and self-awareness. Surprisingly, racoons exhibit many of these same characteristics.

Speaking specifically to their mental capacity, raccoons are closely related to primates in terms of intelligence and problem-solving skills (Pettit, 2010). Being naturally curious creatures with impeccable memories, raccoons are constantly developing new abilities, such as being able to pick locks. They also have tremendous hearing and social skills, and social skills are essential in any leadership capacity, even if their efforts are only focused on leading their nursery to a dumpster.

While many may consider "trash pandas" a nuisance, you can learn from these masked mammalians. For instance, their inherent tenacity and inquisitiveness often leads them to discover new and abundant food sources. These lessons in perseverance, and inquisitorial exploration are ones from which most anyone can benefit, particularly those in leadership positions.

As leaders, fostering a culture of curiosity can be a tremendous benefit. By encouraging employees to seek out new ways of doing things, you can not only ensure that your organization remains relevant, but that it also stays ahead of the curve.

Leading by Example:
Industry-Wide Technical Competencies

Real Life Leaders

Margaret Mead, with her field work and writing got people talking and put anthropology on the map.

Some rare individuals are exceptionally adept with a multitude of skills and abilities. For instance, Leonardo da Vinci is considered not only one of the most talented painters of all time, but also one of the greatest inventors, architects, engineers, and sculptors the world has ever known. Marie Curie was a groundbreaking physicist and chemist. Benjamin Franklin was an inventor, scientist, politician, and author. More recently (perhaps even surprisingly), Steve Martin is an accomplished actor, comedian, writer, and Grammy award winning musician.

Each of these individuals worked hard to cultivate their knowledge, skills, and abilities within their chosen professions. Another such "Renaissance person" was Margaret Mead. Known for studying a wide array of societal issues, such as: anthropology, women's rights, nuclear proliferation, race relations, environmental pollution, and world hunger, Mead (as with the other aforementioned experts) contributed greatly not only to the educational system but to society as a whole (Maguire, 2015).

Although diverse in their achievements, one of the things all these individuals have in common is their quest for continually cultivating and expanding their knowledge. While we may never achieve the greatness for which these people are known, we can strive toward excellence and demonstrate the knowledge, skills, and abilities we do have, as well as staying current with the changes and developments in our industries.

Assess Your Skills: Industry-Wide Technical Competencies

Take a moment to consider what you know about this concept and assess your skills. Indicate your level of agreement with each question.

How competent am I	Very little	Somewhat	Very much
Am I aware of the technology our competitors use, and the technology throughout the industry?			
Do I stay current with technology changes in my industry?			
Am I able to evaluate whether updating to new technology is cost effective and efficient?			
Do I encourage and help my team stay current with industry technologies?			
Do I ensure that my team has access to the necessary technical training and resources?			
Do I attend industry seminars and trade shows?			
Do I network with professionals in my industry?			
Am I the industry expert in my organization?			

7 Tips – What To Do: Industry-Wide Technical Competencies

The following tips will help you become more successful and continually improve your competence in this area. Check those that you need to develop.

☐ 1. Network with other professionals in your industry; list relevant industry resources.

2. Be aware of technological advances that could impact your industry.

3. Log technical questions and industry-related problems when others ask you for assistance. Analyze how you were able to assist them to determine your strengths and weaknesses.

4. Find others in your organization who are strong with regard to the industry skills or knowledge in which you are weak. Ask to observe, work with, and get feedback from them.

5. Try to become the industry expert in your organization in one or more technical areas. Make yourself available as a sounding board for technical ideas.

6. Continually update your knowledge of policies and regulations that apply to your industry area of expertise so that all projects meet industry requirements.

7. Maintain proficiency in your technical area of expertise by remaining involved in your industry and by keeping current on technical literature and developments. When making technical judgments, use pools of available talent to explore and support your ideas.

Development Plan Resources: Industry-Wide Technical Competencies

Build your expertise by reviewing the sources listed below:

Learning and Development Resources
Centrestar Academy. *Developing Global Business and Technical Acumen.* www.centrestar.com
Christensen, C. (2016). *The innovator's dilemma: When new technologies cause great firms to fail.*
Pennington, R. (2013). *Make change work: Staying nimble, relevant, and engaged in a world of constant change.*
Schadler, T., Bernoff, J. & Ask, J. (2014). *The Mobile Mind Shift: Engineer Your Business to Win.*

Organizations that fail to innovate risk extinction.

35

Reflection and Application: Industry-Wide Technical Competencies

Industry technical competence is necessary for every professional. Again, in our printing example, to do the job effectively even the person who runs the printing press should have some understanding of the technology associated with folding and packaging, and his leader should have an awareness of how the competition performs each job.

Remember:

- Stay current with the technology used in your industry.
- Encourage your staff to stay current as well.

The most important concept I learned about this competency is:

_____

_____

_____

To effectively apply this concept to my personal development I plan to:

_____

_____

_____

_____

_____

_____

_____

_____

_____

_____

Keeping one's finger on the technological pulse of one's industry provides an important competitive advantage.

Section III
Build Your Competence

In today's complex, competitive, and changing world, you must show your competencies each day, and you must continue to grow and build your competence, or you risk falling behind.

Building competency has several facets. No one learns everything at once. For example, if you work to increase your conceptual thinking skills, you will improve step by step, but it will take time before you judge yourself as being competent. Even then, things are guaranteed to change. Maybe the nature of your job will change. Or your job tools will change. Or perhaps you will accept a new job, one that necessitates new knowledge and skills. Thus, life-long learning is now the norm.

In this section, we discuss ideas to help you:

- Move from analysis to action, so you take what you learn and put it to practical application and continue to learn.

- Take charge of your professional life by realizing that no one has time for everything, so you must be a critical thinker who sorts what is essential from what is not.

- Realize that unless you make time for professional development, time will pass you by.

- Continue to grow by studying the 35 competencies and formulating new action plans to address your current developmental needs.

- Summarize and own critical takeaways from this book.

Move from Analysis to Action

The competition out there is tough. Organizations can essentially buy the same equipment and use it the same way, but the organization with the best-trained and educated people will produce the best products and services.

- Wesley Donahue[44]

Reading is a valuable way to gain knowledge. This is why schools have textbooks, why online news sites and blogs are popular, and why business and self-help books are a billion-dollar industry. However, reading without reflecting and acting will accomplish little.

To become more accomplished in your field and a more successful leader, you must engage with the material presented here. Question it, think about how it relates to your career and experience, and begin to internalize the concepts.

As with any learning, simply reading without engaging will accomplish little. The level of effort you put forth will determine how much you improve and how close you come to realizing your full potential. You must reflect on what you learn and then apply that knowledge to your career.

How do you do that? You do it by acting, by practicing what you have learned. Act and see what happens. Use your new knowledge to complete a work task and see if you like the results. Were you able to achieve better results? Were you able to do things you had not done before? Did someone else comment on your skill? Learn by practicing your skills. Action is essential to success.

You can also take action by returning to the 35 Competencies and see what you can learn from your new vantage point. Do you better understand what you read now that you have had a chance to use the information in your everyday world?

Be sure to review the list of resources provided in each competency. Have you looked at them? We selected each one from the experience of seeing other people advance by using the information. You can use them to advance as well.

Take Charge of Your Professional Life

Plans are nothing; planning is everything.

– Dwight D. Eisenhower[45]

When you become a critical thinker and a life-long learner you take charge of your professional life, and possibly even your personal life. You become a person who is introspective, who looks at the experiences and knowledge of others, and from that considers what might apply to you and what might not.

You learn to look for patterns of behavior that are helpful and those that are not helpful to create goals that guide your accomplishments, and to weed out what is unimportant in your life.

If you are to continue advancing in today's competitive world, you must also develop the qualities of being flexible and resilient. Life, as they say, happens. This is certainly true in business. You cannot control the world, and sometimes it may feel as though you cannot control your small piece of it, but you can control your response to setbacks and career concerns.

One way to gain some distance from current difficulties is to go back to Competency 13: Flexibility and Resilience. Work through the practice steps and explore the resources for further development. You might also work through Competency 16: Self Direction, because it will help remind you that you are the person in charge of your life.

Make Time for Your Development

You prove what is important to you when you give time to it. You show your loved ones that they are important by giving time to them. You make your work important by giving time to it. You make clients important by sharing time with them. You must do the same for yourself. You must make time for personal and professional growth. Make it a priority.

One way to make time for yourself is to schedule 10 minutes for reflection every morning before you begin your day, and 10 minutes every afternoon or evening before you leave work. In the morning begin by reflecting on your goals for the day. Consider what is important to accomplish, what you are going to prioritize, and what you will do that day to improve your skills. It just takes 10 minutes.

Then, when you are ready to leave work or just before you go to sleep, take another ten minutes to reflect on how your day went. Examine what went well and think about how your planning made the day more productive or how it could have made it even more so.

Think, briefly, about what did not work. Maybe a project ran late, or a target was missed. Reflect on what you can do differently next time to make things run more smoothly.

Establishing a daily habit of setting aside a few minutes for planning and reflection can make a real difference in what you achieve each day.

Continue Growing by Making New Action Plans

While developing your competencies might seem like work, you might not have considered that as you grow and change your world will also change. You will see yourself differently based on your new capabilities, and people will see you differently based what they see you do and on how you respond to them.

Realizing that you are growing and reaping the rewards of that growth is wonderful! But there is always more you can do given the nature of today's world. Do not become complacent and think you are finished learning and growing.

Bask in the glory of the competencies in which you currently excel. But also, go back and review those that need attention. For example, have you avoided financial tasks because you did not feel confident? Now would be the time to realize that you could build your confidence by reviewing Competency 24: Financial Management. Also follow through with the resources suggested. You would not need to become a CPA, but you could be someone who contributes when the subject is money.

Continue your growth by completing a new Competency Action Plan worksheet for the competencies you want to develop now. You might want to skip this step, but when you work through a competency, we advise that you use the worksheet. Because thinking about how developing the skill will help you in your current position is a game changer. It focuses you not just on learning, but on learning how having the competency will help move your career forward. Also, when you are clear on how the competency will help you do a better job, you can pick the resources that will help you most.

Appendix E has some blank Competency Action Plans. Use them!

Key Takeaways from this Book

Going forward, here is what you need to keep in mind as you continue to make decisions and act:

- Continued reflection, self-assessment, and life-long learning are essential if you want to be an effective leader.

- You must have personal and professional goals, both short and long term. Write down those goals. Revisit them every few weeks. Modify them as necessary and keep them fresh in your mind. Know them. Live them.

- Consider using a vision board to reach your goals. This is a board where you put images that help you remember things you want to achieve. For example, if you want a boat, put a picture of the kind of boat you want on your board. Look at that picture every day and remember you are working toward owning it. Want and need that goal. Reach it.

- Understand the 35 leadership competencies as taught in this book and continue to assess your accomplishments in each area. Continue improving your skills by doing new Competency Action Plans.

- Continue to prepare new Competency Action Plans – one per competency – and revisit your action plans as often as you can to remind yourself of what you want to achieve.

- Review the resources discussed in the competencies you are working on, or the compiled list in Appendix D, and choose a new resource to explore.

- Spend a few minutes every morning considering both your goals and your plans for the day. Reflect on the previous day, on what went well and on what you can improved today.

Competency Worksheets

Use the Competency worksheets that follow as a template to formulate and document your thoughts and plans for your first two or three competency areas. Make additional copies of the form as you expand your focus to building and acquiring expertise in all competency areas.

Appendices

Here, you will find the following information:

Appendix A discusses how to use the 35 competencies when working with a multi-rater feedback system.

Appendix B describes how to use the 35 competencies for team and group assessments.

Appendix C has information for educators who want to use this book as a supplementary text. It describes learning activities designed to work with each competency. The book and learning activities can also be used in workshops, seminars, and learn-at-lunch programs.

Appendix D provides a list of all resources discussed in this book.

Appendix E provides blank Competency Action Plan worksheets.

How to Use the 35 Competencies for Multi-Rater Feedback

As many as 90 percent of organizations utilize some form of multi-rater feedback. Studies show that multi-rater feedback assists organizations in improving employee performance in two ways. They provide employees with the opportunity of seeing their performance from different perspectives, and they provide direction for growth.

The Leadership Competency Inventory (LCI) can be used as a development tool to provide ratings across many behaviors. The individuals who do the ratings are categorized by the relationship they have to you. For example, they may be a manager, colleague, or someone who directly or indirectly reports to you.

People who do the ratings are asked to be fair and accurate and to base their ratings on their observations of your performance in specific areas. The resulting report presents the findings of this multi-rater feedback process. It contains your self-ratings and the ratings provided by your co-workers, as well as written feedback provided by those who rate you.

The purpose of the multi-rater feedback survey is to help you explore how you contribute to the success of your organization, and to help you identify opportunities to become more successful and fulfilled in your role. The report shows "the gap," which is the difference between how you rate yourself as compared to the individuals who rated your ability to perform based on specific competencies.

How to Use the 35 Competencies for Team and Group Assessments

The 35 competencies are part of a system that anyone can use to help assess and develop individuals, teams, and groups. While this book focuses on how individuals can use the 35 competencies, you can also use the 35 competencies to assist in identifying the training and development needs of a team or larger group.

In fact, the Leadership Competency Inventory (LCI) is an excellent tool for managers to use when assessing teams and groups. The LCI is an objective tool. When managers are uncertain about the skills or competencies a team or group needs to perform their jobs, the LCI will provide a good starting place.

Managers will also find the LCI useful in response to a request for specific training necessary to deal with a problem that has come to the attention of senior management or Human Resources. In situations like this, what we often find, through inquiry or formal assessment, is that the presented problem may not be the real problem. In other words, the need for development as perceived by others does not always match a group's actual development needs. The data and insights provided through the LCI process clarifies actual needs and gives focus to the training or development program. Our experience shows that this approach to making program recommendations helps strengthen relationships and leads to better outcomes for everyone.

APPENDIX C

How to Use this Book as a Supplementary Text or Seminar Guide

We designed this book for individuals who want to build their leadership capabilities; however, faculty teaching at universities and colleges will also find the book to be an invaluable supplementary text. The book can also be used as a guide for seminars, workshops, and learn-at-lunch programs.

Below are seven examples of active learning assignments that illustrate ways to use the book. Applied in any instructional environment, these lessons can be formally assessed and graded with relevant feedback, which will aid participants in understanding their competencies and developing them.

Learning Activity 1: *Leadership Competencies*

After studying and understanding the 35 competencies, participants select one competency to discuss with the group. With the support of the activity leader, each participant introduces the competency to the group by giving an example – either actual or imagined – that brings the competency to life.

The activity leader encourages the group to explore how mastering the competency might help them and how they can apply it to their industries, jobs, and personal lives.

Learning Activity 2: *Personal Development Plan*

This activity helps participants take control of their own learning and professional development in a structured manner while taking advantage of formal or informal networks, or publicly available information and resources.

Each participant prepares a one or two page Personal Development Plan that the participant then shares with the group. Participant plans address the following information:

1. Identify three competencies you would like to develop.

2. Briefly explain how improving each competency will help you achieve your primary goals.

3. Identify one or more people who could be helpful in your development as a role model or as an informational source. Write down any questions you would like to ask these people.

4. What two or three organizations or work units would you like to learn more about? What specifically would you like to learn?

5. What specific action steps will you take? What are your beginning and ending dates for these actions?

Learning Activity 3: *Competency Resources*

Participants research online resources in the public domain. Further, the resources should have a 90 percent or better positive viewer response and the more people that viewed the resources the better. Examples of appropriate resources are government websites; TedTalks; YouTube; and Vimeo clips.

After participants complete their research, they share their findings with the group.

Learning Activity 4: *Leadership Article Abstract*

Participants select an article about leadership that is of interest to them and also relevant to the group. They read the article and prepare a one-page abstract for sharing with the group.

In the abstract, participants identify which of the 35 competencies are the focus of the article, briefly explain why the ideas in the article are important, summarize the content in a clear and concise manner, and discuss the practical applications, if any, of the ideas for aspiring leaders.

Learning Activity 5: *On-The-Job Leadership Development Activities*

Organize participants into groups. Assign each group one of the following five competency clusters to brainstorm and list on-the-job activities that can be implemented in their work unit or organizations to help individuals build competence.

- Resource Management
- Technical Competence
- Supervisory Management
- Organizational Leadership
- Technical Acumen

Learning Activity 6: *Personal Interview of a Leader*

Each participant interviews someone to whom they have access and whom they consider to be an exemplary leader. Using the five competency clusters as a basis for an interview, the interviewer asks the leader how the person gained experience in each area, what critical events occurred, what they learned from those events, and recommended actions for aspiring leaders. Each participant then shares what was learned in the interview with the group.

Learning Activity 7: *Scavenger Hunt for Images of Exemplary Leadership*

Teams, using the 35 competencies as a guide, take or find twenty-four photographs or images that depict what the students believe are examples of exemplary leadership.

Based on originality and creativity, select and share the best images for a brief PowerPoint Presentation to the group. Form a collage of five images selected by each team, and add captions explaining the rationale for each selection.

Coach participants to take photos in a respectful and professional manner, and to use photos and images in compliance with copyright law.

APPENDIX D

Recommended Additional Resources

Following is an alphabetical compilation of all the resources recommended in this book:

5 simple ways to improve your writing. (2012). Forbes. Available from, http://www.forbes.com/sites/dailymuse/2012/05/22/5-simple-ways-to-improve-your-writing/

Aguilar, E. (2020). *Coaching for equity: Conversations that change practice.*

Baggini, J. & Fosl, P. (2020). *A philosopher's toolkit: A compendium of philosophical concepts and methods.*

Bennis, W. (2009). *On becoming a leader.* Perseus publishing.

Bensoussan, B.E. & Fleisher, C.S. (2015). *Analysis without paralysis: 12 tools to make better strategic decisions.*

Berman, K. (2013). *Financial intelligence: A manager's guide to knowing what the numbers really mean.*

Bogino, D. (2011). *Conceptual Thinking (1.5 minute introduction).* Available at, https://www.youtube.com/watch?v=Na2o3ZEoCkM

Bolton, R. (1986). *People skills: How to assert yourself, listen to others, and resolve conflicts.*

Bridges, W. (2017). *Managing transitions: making the most of change.*

Brown, J. (2012). *Systems thinking strategy: The new way to understand your business and drive performance.*

Browning, G. (2013). *The power of conceptual thinking to strengthen your leadership. Inc.* Available at, http://www.inc.com/geil-browning/strengthen-leadership-conceptual-thinking.html

Brynteson, R. (2010). *Once upon a complex time: Using stories to understand systems.*

Canales, B. (2019). *Enneagram in relationships: Understand your personality type and other personalities to build healthy relationships.*

Carnegie, D. (1998). *How to win friends & influence people.*

Caspersen, D. & Elffers, J. (2015). *Changing the conversation: The 17 principles of conflict resolution.*

Centrestar Academy. Multiple Resources – Visit: www.centrestar.com

Chaffee, J. (2018). *Thinking critically.*

Chaffee, J. (2014). *Critical thinking, thoughtful writing.*

Chenier, N.J. (2005). *Chenier's Practical Math Application Guide: For Do-it-yourselfers, Trades People, Students, etc.*

Christensen, C. (2016). *The innovator's dilemma: When new technologies cause great firms to fail.*

Cialdini, R.B. (2021). *Influence: The psychology of persuasion.*

Covey, S.R. (2020). *The 7 habits of highly effective people: Powerful lessons in personal change.*

Coach K. Quotes - Visit: http://coachk.com

Coburn, D. (2014). *Networking is not working: Stop collecting business cards and start making meaningful connections.*

Cohan, A. (2017). *Influence without authority.*

Colan, L.J. (2008). *Engaging the hearts and minds of all your employees: How to ignite passionate performance for better business results.*

Colan, L.J. (2017). *The 5 coaching habits of excellent leaders.*

Conklin, T. (2019). *The 5 principles of human performance.*

Conn, C. (2019). *Bulletproof problem solving: the one skill that changes everything.*

Cook, S. (2011). *Customer care excellence: how to create an effective customer focus.*

Costa, A.L. & Kallick, B. (2009). *Learning and leading habits of the mind: 16 essential characteristics for success.*

Covey, S.R. (2020). *The 7 habits of highly effective people: Powerful lessons in personal change.*

Delaney, D. (2013). *New business networking: How to effectively grow your business networks using on-line and off-line methods.*

Doerr, J. (2018). *Measure what matters: How google, bono, and the gates foundation rock the world with okrs.*

Donahue, W. (2021). *Unlocking Lean Six Sigma.*

Duhigg, C. (2014). *The power of habit: Why we do what we do in life and business.*

Dungy, T. (2019). *The soul of a team: AS modern day fable for winning teamwork.*

Espinoza, C. & Ukleja, M. (2016). *Managing the millennials: discover the core competencies for managing today's workforce.*

Fisher, R. & Ury, W.L. (2011). *Getting to yes: Negotiating agreement without giving in.*

Fournier, C. (2017). *The manager's path: A guide for tech leaders navigating growth and change.*

Friedman, V. (2009). *50 free resources that will improve your writing skills.* Available at, http://www.smashingmagazine.com/2009/06/50-free-resources-that-will-improve-your-writing-skills/

Fullan, M. (2020). *Leading in a culture of change.*

Fuller, P. (2020). *The leader's guide to unconscious bias.*

Gavin, P. (2021). *The workplace guide to time management: Best practices to maximize productivity.*

Gallo, A. (2017). *Hbr guide to dealing with conflict.*

Gerber, M. (2004). *The e-myth revisited: Why most small businesses fail and what to do about it.*

Gitomer, J. (1998). *Customer satisfaction is worthless, customer loyalty is priceless.*

Glei, J.K. & 99U. (2013). *Manage your day-to-day: Build your routine, find your focus, and sharpen your creative mind.*

Goodrich, R. (2021). *SWOT Analysis: Examples, templates & definition.* Retrieved from, http://www.businessnewsdaily.com/4245-swot-analysis.html

Green, J. (2018). *The procrastination fix: 36 strategies proven to cure laziness and improve productivity: Daily training for mental toughness and self discipline.*

Grenny, J. & Patterson, K. (2013). *Influencer: The new science of leading change.*

Hackman, R. (2002). *Leading teams: Setting the stage for great performances.*

Haden, J. (2015). *9 habits of people who build extraordinary relationships.* Available from, http://www.inc.com/jeff-haden/9-habits-of-people-who-build-extraordinary-relationships.html

Hall, B. (2019). *Self-Discipline.*

Hagemann, B. (2017). *Leading with vision: The leader's blueprint for creating a compelling vision and engaging the workforce.*

Health, C. & Heath, D. (2020). *Switch: How to change things when change is hard.*

Heath, C. & Heath, D. (2020). *Decisive: How to make better choices in life and work.*

Horowitz, B. (2019). *What you do is who you are: How to create your business culture.*

Hyatt, M. (2020). *The vision-driven leader: 10 questions to focus your efforts, energize your team, and scale your business.*

Hooker, J. (2010). *Business ethics as rational choice.*

Jackson, K. (n.d.). *What is problem solving?* Available at, https://www.mindtools.com/pages/article/newTMC_00.htm

James, G. (2012). *Be customer-focused: 4 basic tactics. Inc.* Available at, http://www.inc.com/geoffrey-james/be-customer-focused-4-basic-tactics.html

Journal of Technology Management & Innovation. http://www.jotmi.org/index.php/GT

Joy, M. (2020). *Getting relationships right: How to build resilience and thrive in life, love, and work.*

Kahn Academy. *Free basic computer and other tutorials.* Visit www.khanacademy.org

Kahneman, D. (2013). *Thinking, fast and slow.*

Knight, J. & Thomas, R. (2012). *Project management for profit: A failsafe guide to keeping projects on track and on budget.*

Kosterlitz, A. (2019). *Fearless feedback: A guide for coaching leaders to see themselves more clearly and galvanize growth.*

Krzyzewski, M. (2001). *Leading with the heart: Coach k's successful strategies for basketball, business, and life.*

Kotter, J.P. (2012). *Leading change.*

Larson, C. & LaFasto, F.M.J. (2015). *Teamwork: What must go right/what can go wrong.*

Lippitt, M. (2019). *Situational mindsets: Targeting what matters when it matters.*

Magretta, J. (2011). *Understanding Michael Porter: The essential guide to competition and strategy.*

Manktelow, J. (n.d.). *Mission and vision statements: Unleashing the power of purpose.* Available at, https://www.mindtools.com/pages/article/newLDR_90.htm

Manning, H. & Bodine, K. (2012). *Outside in: The power of putting customers at the center of your business.*

Mantle, M. W. and Lichty, R. (2019). *Managing the unmanageable: Rules, tools, and insights for managing software people and teams.*

Martin, C. (2014). *Moral decision making: How to approach everyday ethics.*

Maxwell, J.C. (2013). *The 5 levels of leadership: Proven steps to maximize your potential.*

McClean, D.R. (2020). *Strategic planning: As simple as A, B, C.*

Meadows, D. (2021). *Summary and analysis of thinking in systems: A primer.*

Mitchell, B. (2017). *The conflict resolution phrase book.*

Mor Barak, M.E. (2013). *Managing diversity: Toward a globally inclusive workplace.*

Morgan, B. (2019). *The customer of the future: 10 guiding principles for winning tomorrow's business.*

Moriarty, T. (2019). *The productive leadership™ system: Maximizing organizational reliability.*

Navarro, J. & Karlins, M. (2018). *What every BODY is saying: An ex-FBI agent's guide to speed-reading people.*

Olsen, E. (2011). *Strategic planning kit for dummies.*

Olson, A.K. & Simerson, B.K. (2015). *Leading with strategic thinking: Four ways effective leaders gain insight, drive change, and get results.*

Page, S. (2018). *The model thinker: What you need to know to make data work for you.*

Pearse, M. & Dunwoody, M. (2013). *Learning that never ends: Qualities of a lifelong learner.*

Pink, D. (2018). *A whole new mind: Why right-brainers will rule the future.*

Provost, F. & Fawcett, T. (2013). *Data science for business: What you need to know about data mining and data-analytic thinking.*

Provost, G., & Grimes, P. (2019). *100 Ways to improve your writing: Proven professional techniques for writing with style and power.*

Pennington, R. (2013). *Make change work: Staying nimble, relevant, and engaged in a world of constant change.*

Porter, M.E. (2008). *On competition, updated and expanded edition.*

Portny, S.E. (2020). *Project management for dummies.*

Project Management Institute (PMI). (2013). *A guide to the project management body of knowledge: (PMBOK(R) Guide.*

Pynes, J.E. (2013). *Human resources management for public and nonprofit organizations: a strategic approach.*

Rogers, P., Blenko, M.W., & Davis-Peccoud, J. (2012). *Bad decisions in history: Cautionary tales.* Available at, http://www.bain.com/publications/articles/bad-decisions-in-history-cautionary-tales.aspx

Roser, C, (2021). *All about pull production: Designing, implementing, and maintaining kanban, conwip, and other pull systems in lean production.*

Ross, H., Verclas, K., and Levine, A. (2009). *Managing technology to meet your mission: A strategy guide for non-profit leaders.*

Rothwell, W., Donahue, W., Park, J. (2001). *Creating in-house sales training and development programs*

Sarder, R. (2011). *Learning: Steps to becoming a passionate lifelong learner.*

Schwarzman, S. (2019). *What it takes: Lessons in the pursuit of excellence.*

Siciliano, G. (2014). *Finance for nonfinancial managers.*

Snarski, R.D. (2018). *Communicating Clearly in the Information Age.*

Snell, S.A. & Bohlander, G.W. (2012). *Managing human resources.*

Stanier, M. (2016). *The coaching habit: say less, ask more & change the way you lead forever*

Stevens, A. (2013). *Turn your dreams and wants into achievable SMART goals! A comprehensive manual on effective goal-setting for entrepreneurs, managers, and parents.*

Stokes, A. (2015). *Is this thing on? A friendly guide to everything digital for newbies, technophobes, and the kicking & screaming.*

Struck, W., & White, E. (2021). *The elements of style.*

Sullivan, D. (2020). *Who not how: The formula to achieve bigger goals through accelerating teamwork.*

Su, T. (n.d.). *9 steps to be decisive.* Available at, http://thinksimplenow.com/clarity/9-steps-to-be-decisive/

SystemsThinker.com. *Systems thinking.* Available at, http://www.systemsthinker.com/interests/systemsthinking/

Telford, O. (2019). *Mindfulness: The remarkable truth behind meditation and being present in your life.*

Thinknetic (2021). *Critical thinking in a nutshell: How to become an independent thinker and make intelligent decisions.*

Thomas, J. (2020). *Thinking differently: How to thrive using your nonlinear creative thinking.*

Throness, T. (2017). *Power of people skills: How to eliminate 90% of your hr problems and dramatically increase team and company morale and performance. Organizations: A strategic approach.*

Tracy, B. (2017). *Eat that frog!: 21 great ways to stop procrastinating and get more done in less time.*

Trott, D. (2016). *One plus one equals three: A masterclass in creative thinking.*

Tsaousides, T. (2015). *The 7 habits of highly ineffective people: Are you one of them?* Psychology Today. Retrieved from, https://www.psychologytoday.com/blog/smashing-the-brainblocks/201508/the-7-habits-highly-ineffective-people

Tuckman, B. (n.d.). *Forming, storming, norming and performing in groups.* Retrieved from, http://infed.org/mobi/bruce-w-tuckman-forming-storming-norming-and-performing-in-groups/

Tuhovsky, I. (2018). *The science of interpersonal relations.*

Vogel, T. (2014). *Breakthrough thinking: A guide to creative thinking and idea generation.*

Voss, C. (2016). *Never split the difference: Negotiating as if your life depended On it.*

Weise, M. (2020). *Long life learning: Preparing for jobs that don't even exist yet.*

Wempen, F. (2015). *Digital literacy for dummies.*

Wilson, G. (2020). *Beginners guide to computer literacy: A well written guide on the computer basics, component, shortcuts and its uses.*

Wood, J. (2019). *The interpersonal communication: Everyday encounters.*

Yeh, C. (2018). *Blitzscaling: The lightning-fast path to building massively valuable companies.*

Young, K.S. & Travis, H.P. (2017). *Oral communication: Skills, choices, and consequences.*

Zemke, R. & Raines, C. (2013). *Generations at work: Managing the clash of boomers, Gen Xers, and Gen Yers in the workplace.*

Zenger, J. & Stinnett, K. (2010). *The extraordinary coach: How the best leaders help others grow.*

Appendix E

Blank Competency Action Plan Worksheets

Here are a few blank Competency Action Plan worksheets. Recall, we introduced the worksheet in Section I: Plan Your Career. If you are unsure of how to use the worksheet, please review the information in Section I.

Use the worksheet to plan the future you want to have. Depending on how many competencies you want to improve, you may want to make photocopies.

Competency: _____

Briefly describe how improvement in this competency will help you achieve important results or better meet your job responsibilities.

_____

_____

_____

_____

_____

_____

_____

List courses, books, and independent study opportunities that could help you develop this competency.

_____

_____

_____

_____

_____

_____

_____

_____

_____

_____

_____

_____

Identify one or more people who could help you, either as a role model or source of information. Write any questions you want to ask each person.

_____

_____

_____

_____

_____

_____

_____

_____

_____

_____

_____

_____

_____

What specific steps will you take?	Start Date	Finished
_____	_____	_____
_____	_____	_____
_____	_____	_____
_____	_____	_____
_____	_____	_____
_____	_____	_____
_____	_____	_____

Competency: _____

Briefly describe how improvement in this competency will help you achieve important results or better meet your job responsibilities.

_____

_____

_____

_____

_____

_____

_____

List courses, books, and independent study opportunities that could help you develop this competency.

_____

_____

_____

_____

_____

_____

_____

_____

_____

_____

_____

_____

Identify one or more people who could help you, either as a role model or source of information. Write any questions you want to ask each person.

_____

_____

_____

_____

_____

_____

_____

_____

_____

_____

_____

_____

_____

_____

_____

What specific steps will you take?	Start Date	Finished
_____	_____	_____
_____	_____	_____
_____	_____	_____
_____	_____	_____
_____	_____	_____
_____	_____	_____
_____	_____	_____

Competency: _____

Briefly describe how improvement in this competency will help you achieve important results or better meet your job responsibilities.

_____

_____

_____

_____

_____

_____

_____

List courses, books, and independent study opportunities that could help you develop this competency.

_____

_____

_____

_____

_____

_____

_____

_____

_____

_____

_____

_____

Identify one or more people who could help you, either as a role model or source of information. Write any questions you want to ask each person.

_____

_____

_____

_____

_____

_____

_____

_____

_____

_____

_____

_____

_____

What specific steps will you take?	Start Date	Finished

Competency: _____

Briefly describe how improvement in this competency will help you achieve important results or better meet your job responsibilities.

_____

_____

_____

_____

_____

_____

_____

List courses, books, and independent study opportunities that could help you develop this competency.

_____

_____

_____

_____

_____

_____

_____

_____

_____

_____

_____

_____

Identify one or more people who could help you, either as a role model or source of information. Write any questions you want to ask each person.

_____

_____

_____

_____

_____

_____

_____

_____

_____

_____

_____

_____

_____

What specific steps will you take?	Start Date	Finished
_____	_____	_____
_____	_____	_____
_____	_____	_____
_____	_____	_____
_____	_____	_____
_____	_____	_____
_____	_____	_____
_____	_____	_____

Competency: _____

Briefly describe how improvement in this competency will help you achieve important results or better meet your job responsibilities.

_____

_____

_____

_____

_____

_____

_____

_____

List courses, books, and independent study opportunities that could help you develop this competency.

_____

_____

_____

_____

_____

_____

_____

_____

_____

_____

_____

_____

Identify one or more people who could help you, either as a role model or source of information. Write any questions you want to ask each person.

_____

_____

_____

_____

_____

_____

_____

_____

_____

_____

_____

_____

_____

What specific steps will you take?	Start Date	Finished
_____	_____	_____
_____	_____	_____
_____	_____	_____
_____	_____	_____
_____	_____	_____
_____	_____	_____
_____	_____	_____

Quote Sources

1) Frost, D.B. (2013). *John F. Kennedy in Quotations: A Topical Dictionary, with Sources*. Jefferson, NC: McFarland.

2) Meyer, P.J. (n.d.). Retrieved from, http://www.brainyquote.com/quotes/keywords/planning.html#SUU05W6Ewjgv3uZx.99

3) Ramsey, D. (2011). *EntreLeadership: 20 years of practical business wisdom from the trenches*. Brentwood, TN: Howard Books.

4) Arden, P. (n.d.). Retrieved from, http://www.brainyquote.com/quotes/keywords/tools.html#fE1OYMb2XkvPMKYT.99

5) Gates, B. (n.d.). Retrieved from, http://www.brainyquote.com/quotes/keywords/tools.html#fE1OYMb2XkvPMKYT.99

6) Ballmer. S. (2005). Retrieved from, http://news.microsoft.com/2005/02/17/steve-ballmer-aacis-unlimited-potential-grant-announcement/

7) Shingo, S. (n.d.). Retrieved from, http://www.quotegarden.com/lean-manufacturing.html

8) Covey, S. (1989). *The seven habits of highly effective people: Restoring the character of ethics*.

9) Jobs, S. (n.d.). Retrieved from, http://www.brainyquote.com/quotes/quotes/s/stevejobs416921.html

10)   Emerson, R.W. (n.d.). Retrieved from, http://www.ranker.com/list/notable-and-famous-property-quotes/reference?var=2&utm_expid=16418821-169.cy7ItobhRmC61Q5VlyGNgw.1&utm_referrer=https%3A%2F%2F

11)   Alessandra, T. (n.d.). Retrieved from, http://izquotes.com/quote/337197

12)   Roosevelt, E. (n.d.). Retrieved from, http://quoteinvestigator.com/2012/04/30/no-one-inferior/

13)   Drucker, P. (2003). *Essential Drucker: Management, the individual and society*.

14)   Ford, H. (n.d.). Retrieved from, http://www.brainyquote.com/quotes/authors/h/henry_ford.html

15)   Robbins, A. (n.d.). Retrieved from, http://www.goodreads.com/quotes/152284-to-effectively-communicate-we-must-realize-that-we-are-all

16)   King, S. (2000). *On writing: A memoir of the craft*.

17) Parton, D. (1997). Retrieved from, http://quoteinvestigator.com/2011/07/03/inspire-dream-leader/

18) Deming, W.E. (n.d.). Retrieved from, http://www.brainyquote.com/quotes/quotes/w/wedwardsd133510.html

19) Tzu, S. (490 B.C.). Retrieved from, http://changingminds.org/disciplines/warfare/art_war/sun_tzu_6-6.htm

20) Shaw, G.B. (n.d.). Retrieved from, http://www.inspirationalstories.com/quotes/george-bernard-shaw-im-only-a-beer-teetotaler-not-a/

21) Covey, S. (n.d.). Retrieved from, http://izquotes.com/quote/340910

22) Byron, L. (n.d.). Retrieved from, http://www.brainyquote.com/quotes/quotes/l/lordbyron161971.html

23) Churchill, W. (n.d.). Retrieved from, http://www.quotationspage.com/quote/39728.html

24) Adams, S. (n.d.). Retrieved from, http://www.famousquotesabout.com/quote/You-don_t-have-to/520322

25) Wild, O. (n.d.). Retrieved from, http://izquotes.com/quote/198063

26) Einstein, A. (n.d.). Retrieved from, http://www.goodreads.com/quotes/84604-setting-an-example-is-not-the-main-means-of-influencing

27) Buddha, as translated by Goddard. (n.d.). Retrieved from, http://fakebuddhaquotes.com/whatever-words-we-utter-should-be-chosen-with-care/

28) Lombardi, V. (n.d.). Retrieved from, http://www.sayingsnquotes.com/quotations-by-subject/leadership-quotes-and-sayings-8/

29) Confucius. (n.d.). Retrieved from, http://izquotes.com/quote/317196

30) Antoine de Saint-Exupery. (n.d.). Retrieved from, https://www.goodreads.com/quotes/87476-a-goal-without-a-plan-is-just-a-wish

31) Kiyosaki, R. (n.d.). Retrieved from, http://www.evancarmichael.com/library/robert-kiyosaki/Robert-Kiyosaki-Quotes.html

32) Gates, B. (n.d.). Retrieved from, http://www.brainyquote.com/quotes/quotes/b/billgates122131.html

33) Ayivor, I. (2014). *The great handbook of quotes*

34) Bennis, W. (n.d.) Retrieved from, https://www.brainyquote.com/quotes/warren_bennis_121713

35) Burchard, B. (n.d.). Retrieved from, http://www.brainyquote.com/quotes/quotes/b/brendonbur487222.html

36) Tzu, S. (n.d.). Retrieved from, http://thinkexist.com/quotation/strategy_without_tactics_is_the_slowest_route_to/220091.html

37) Terry, B. (n.d.). Retrieved from, http://thinkexist.com/quotation/no_business_in_the_world_has_ever_made_more_money/200047.html

38) King, M. (n.d.). Retrieved from, http://www.beliefnet.com/inspiration/2010/01/martin-luther-king-quotes.aspx?p=21

39) Kennedy, J. (n.d.). Retrieved from, https://www.brainyquote.com/quotes/john_f_kennedy_121068

40) Roosevelt, T. (n.d.). Retrieved from, The nation behaves well if it treats the natural resources as assets which it must turn over to the next generation increased, and not impaired, in value

41) Jefferson, T. (n.d.) Retrieved from, https://www.monticello.org/site/research-and-collections/i-am-great-believer-luckspurious-quotation

42) Kass, L. (n.d.). Retrieved from, http://www.brainyquote.com/quotes/quotes/l/leonkass282479.html

43) R. Buckminister Fuller. (2015). Retrieved from, https://www.bfi.org/ideaindex/projects/2015/greenwave

44) Donahue, W. (n.d.). Penn State University / CentreStar, Inc.

45) Eisenhower, D.D. (n.d.). Retrieved from, http://www.brainyquote.com/quotes/quotes/d/dwightdei149111.html

References

"8 examples of evolution in action." (2011). Retrieved from, http://listverse. com/2011/11/19/8-examples-of-evolution-in-action/

Alain, P. (2012). *Leadership and 10 Great Leaders from History*. Retrieved from, https://www.industryleadersmagazine.com/leadership-and-10-great-leaders-from-history/

Ali, A., Baby, B., & Vijayan, R. (2019). *From Desert to Medicine: A Review of Camel Genomics and Therapeutic Products. Frontiers in Genetics*, 10. https:// doi. org/10.3389/fgene.2019.00017

Arizona State University (ASU). (n.d.). Retrieved from, https://askabiologist.asu. edu/animals-tundra

"Bar-tailed godwit". (n.d.). Retrieved from, http://nzbirdsonline.org.nz/species/bar-tailed-godwit

Beekman, M., & Oldroyd, B. P. (2018). *Different bees, different needs: how nest-site requirements have shaped the decision-making processes in homeless honeybees (Apis spp.). Philosophical Transactions of the Royal Society B: Biological Sciences*, 373(1746), 20170010. https://doi.org/ 10.1098/rstb.2017.0010

Belfield, L. (2018). *Cultural Diversity: Imagine All the People*. Retrieved from, https://www.kaplanuniversity.edu/news-resources/what-is-cultural-diversity/

Broughton, K. (n.d.). *Dr. Martin Luther King Jr. The Writer*. Retrieved from, http:// bigthink.com/Resurgence/dr-martin-luther-king-jr-the-writer

Branson, R. (2013). *Richard Branson on the importance of creative thinking*. Entrepreneur. Retrieved from, http://www.entrepreneur.com/article/225866

Choi, C.Q. (2009). *10 animals that use tools*. Retrieved from, http://news. nationalgeographic.com/news/2009/12/091214-octopus-carries-coconuts-coconut-carrying.html

Colvin, G. (2011). *Zhang Ruimin: Management's next icon*. Fortune. Retrieved from, http://fortune.com/2011/07/15/zhang-ruimin-managements-next-icon/

Creative Commons. (2009). *Problem solving animals*. Retrieved from, http:// cognitivepsychology.wikidot.com/problem-solving:animals

CV Tech. (n.d.). *Identifying occupational competencies*. Retrieved from, http:// portal.cvtech.edu/os/Core_Curriculum_CD/AGMECH/UB/B3_3.PDF

Devlin, K. (2010). *Babies change their cry to signify if they are hungry or in pain.* Retrieved from, http://www.telegraph.co.uk/news/health/news/7316407/Babies-change-their-cry-to-signify-if-they-are-hungry-sad-or-in-pain.html

Dictionary.com. (n.d.). *Conceptual.* Retrieved from, http://dictionary.reference.com/browse/conceptual?s=t

Donahue, W. (1996). *A descriptive analysis of perceived importance of leadership competencies to practicing electrical engineers in central Pennsylvania.* Doctoral Dissertation. Penn State University.

Donahue, W., Woodley, K., Park, J. (2010). *Leadership Competency Inventory and Individual Development Plan. Penn State Management Development.* Portions of this document used under license.

Dray, K. (2015). *Decoding baby's cries: What your little one's tears really mean.* Retrieved from, http://www.closeronline.co.uk/2015/07/decoding-babys-cries-what-your-little-ones-tears-really-mean

Emancipation Proclamation. (n.d.). Information and Articles About the Emancipation Proclamation, issued by President Abraham Lincoln during the American Civil War. Retrieved from, http://www.historynet.com/emancipation-proclamation

Feigenbaum, E. (2015). *The value of diversity in the workplace.* Retrieved from, http://smallbusiness.chron.com/value-diversity-workplace-3035.html

Flanders, L., & Utterback, D. (1985). *The management excellence inventory: a tool for management development.* Public Administration Review, 45(3), 403-410.

Former Ritz Carlton President Horst Schulze Talks About The New Frontier In Luxury Hotels. (2012). *Forbes.* Available from: https://www.forbes.com/sites/katiebell/2012/05/03/horst-schulze-on-the-new-frontier-in-luxury-hotels/#4014c78766ef

Florida Aquarium. (n.d.). Retrieved from, www.flaquarium.org

Gardner, Howard. (2006). *Multiple Intelligences: New Horizons in Theory and Practice*, and see also https://www.thoughtco.com/interpersonal-intelligence-8091

Gieling, E. T., Nordquist, *R. E., & van der Staay, F. J. (2011, March). Assessing learning and memory in pigs. Animal cognition.* https://www.ncbi.nlm.nih.gov/pmc/articles/PMC3040303/

Grenny, J. (2012). *Four reasons why leaders lack influence.* Forbes. Retrieved from, http://www.forbes.com/sites/josephgrenny/2012/12/10/four-reasons-why-leaders-lack-influence/

Heath, A. (2017). *Mark Zuckerberg explains Facebook's secrets for acquiring companies*. Business Insider. Retrieved from, http://www.businessinsider.com/mark-zuckerberg-explains-facebooks-acquisition-strategy-2017-1

Helft, M. (2014). *Google's Larry Page: The most ambitious CEO in the universe*. Fortune. Retrieved from, http://fortune.com/2014/11/13/googles-larry-page-the-most-ambitious-ceo-in-the-universe/

Holland, J. (2015). *Surprise: Elephants comfort upset friends*. National Geographic. Retrieved from, http://news.nationalgeographic.com/news/2014/02/140218-asian-elephants-empathy-animals-science-behavior/

Holmes, K. (2012). *Human Resources Q&A: What managers and supervisors need to know about HR*. Retrieved from, https://charityvillage.com/Content.aspx?topic=Human_Resources_Q_A_What_managers_and_supervisors_need_to_know_about_HR&last=678#.VlMQZb_Xblg

How to be decisive. (n.d.). Retrieved from, http://www.wikihow.com/Be-Decisive

Independent. (1996). *Sperm whales follow leader to death on beach*. Retrieved from, http://www.independent.co.uk/news/sperm-whales-follow-leader-to-death-on-beach-1326377.html

Jagielski, P. M., Dey, C. J., Gilchrist, H. G., Richardson, E. S., Love, O. P., & Semeniuk, C. A. D. (2021, April 7). *Polar bears are inefficient predators of seabird eggs. Royal Society Open Science*. https://royalsocietypublishing.org/doi/full/10.1098/rsos.210391#d1e1749

Jarrard, B. (2012). *Conceptual thinking*. Retrieved from, http://www.mindwerx.com/blogs/bill-jarrard/2012/10/08/conceptual-thinking

Kaplan, M. (2009). *"Bizarre" octopuses carry coconuts as instant shelters*. **National Geographic**. Retrieved from, http://news.nationalgeographic.com/news/2009/12/091214-octopus-carries-coconuts-coconut-carrying.html

King, M. (2019). *The good neighbor: the life and work of Fred Rogers. Thorndike Press*.

Lau, E. (2013). *Why and where is teamwork important?* **Forbes**. Retrieved from, http://www.forbes.com/sites/quora/2013/01/23/why-and-where-is-teamwork-important/

Lehrer, J. (2011). *Steve Jobs: "Technology Alone is not Enough."* **The New Yorker**. Retrieved from, http://www.newyorker.com/news/news-desk/steve-jobs-technology-alone-is-not-enough

Mahatma Gandhi Leadership Profile. (2016). Retrieved from, http://www.leadershipgeeks.com/gandhi-leadership/

Maguire, K. (2015). *Margaret Mead Contributions to Contemporary Education.* *Springer.*

Meyer, P.J. (n.d.a). *Success is not a destination – it is a personal journey.* Retrieved from, https://www.pauljmeyer.com/

Meyer, P.J. (n.d.b). *Adopt a "Do it Now!" attitude because NOW is the time to succeed!* Retrieved from, https://www.pauljmeyer.com/

Mott, M. (2005). *Did animals sense tsunami was coming?* Retrieved from, http://news.nationalgeographic.com/news/2005/01/0104_050104_tsunami_animals.html

Nisen, M. (2013). *Google's Larry Page Talks about His Leadership Philosophy.* **Business Insider**. Retrieved from, http://www.businessinsider.com/larry-page-management-secrets-2013-1

Nolop, B. (2014). *Why Michael Bloomberg is My Executive Role Model.* **Wall Street Journal**. Retrieved from, https://blogs.wsj.com/experts/2014/04/30/why-michael-bloomberg-is-my-executive-role-model/

Office of Personnel Management (OPM), Human Resource Development Group, Office of Executive and Management Policy. (1995). *Matrix of characteristics and instruments (unpublished analysis report).* Washington, DC.

Perryman, R. J., Venables, S. K., Tapilatu, R. F., Marshall, A. D., Brown, C., & Franks, D. W. (2019). *Social preferences and network structure in a population of reef manta rays. Behavioral Ecology and Sociobiology*, 73(8). https://doi.org/ 10.1007/s00265-019-2720-x

Poh, M. (n.d.). *6 ways to unleash creativity in the workplace.* Retrieved from, http://www.hongkiat.com/blog/unleash-creativity-workplace/

Problem Solving. (n.d.). Retrieved from, http://www.skillsyouneed.com/ips/problem-solving.html

Rao, M. S. (2012). *Myths and Truths About Soft Skills.* T+D, 66(5), 48-51.

Rappleye, E. (2015). *5 lessons from the leadership of Ford CEO Alan Mulally.* Retrieved from, http://www.beckershospitalreview.com/hospital-management-administration/5-lessons-from-the-leadership-of-ford-ceo-alan-mulally.html

Rothwell, W., Donahue, W., & Park, J. (2002). *Creating In-House Sales Development Programs.* Greenwood Publishers.

Scarf, D., & Colombo, M. (2019, December 19). *Columban Simulation Project 2.0: Numerical Competence and Orthographic Processing in Pigeons and Primates.* *Frontiers.* https://www.frontiersin.org/articles/ 10.3389/fpsyg.2019.03017/full

Schoemaker, P. (2012). *6 habits of true strategic thinkers*. **Inc**. Retrieved from, http://www.inc.com/paul-schoemaker/6-habits-of-strategic-thinkers.html

Six Leadership Traits of Winston Churchill. (2015). Retrieved from, http://www.supplychain247.com/article/six_leadership_traits_of_sir_winston_churchill

Smith, K. (2018). *Martin Luther King Jr. Tribute*. Retrieved from, https://www.dopeeramagazine.com/single-post/2018/01/15/Martin-Luther-King-Jr-Tribute

Smithsonian Channel. (2014). *Crazy monster frogs*. Retrieved from, http://www.smithsonianchannel.com/shows/crazy-monster-frogs/0/3412156

Staub, R. (2008). *Flexibility, principles balance true leadership*. Retrieved from, http://www.bizjournals.com/triad/stories/2008/06/23/smallb3.html?page=all

Steinbeck, J. (1937). *Of mice and men*.

Top 10 cases of animals saving humans. (2010). Retrieved from, http://listverse.com/2010/03/14/top-10-cases-of-animals-saving-humans/

The Miracle Worker, https://en.wikipedia.org/wiki/The_Miracle_Worker_(1962_film)

The University of Sydney (UOS). (2010). *Problem-solving ants inspire next generation of algorithms*. Retrieved from, http://sydney.edu.au/news/84.html?newscategoryid=2&newsstoryid=6165

Walker, M. (2012). *Birds hold "funerals" for dead*. Retrieved from, http://www.bbc.co.uk/nature/19421217

Watanabe, K. (2009). *The importance of problem-solving*. Retrieved from, http://www.huffingtonpost.com/ken-watanabe/the-importance-of-problem_b_190514.html

Wharton University of Pennsylvania (WUP). (2010). *Lessons in Leadership from the Life of the Prophet Muhammad*.

Yakowicz, W. (2013). *How American Express's CEO Learned to Lead 70,000 Employees*. **Inc**. Retrieved from, https://www.inc.com/will-yakowicz/american-express-kenneth-chenault-how-to-lead-70000-employees.html

Index

A

B

G

H

Q

R

[Created with TExtract / www.TExtract.com]

About the Author

Wesley E. Donahue, PhD, PE, PMP®

As a business owner, engineer, manager, and now an educator, I have always thought of myself as being in the business of helping other people succeed. But like you, at each step of the way I had to learn, and I had to put that learning into action. This book speaks from the voice of experience.

As for my background, I am a professor of Management Development and Education at Penn State University. In this capacity, I am engaged in top-ranked graduate research and programing in learning and performance and lead a successful online graduate program in organization development and change. I am also president of Centrestar, Inc. a firm that offers a unique and straightforward approach for professionals to assess their leadership skills, develop personalized roadmaps for success, and access on-demand micro-learning courses that get results. View our courses at: www.centrestar.com

Before that, I was Director of Penn State Management Development Programs and Services, which provided education and training services to business and industry clients around the world. Prior to that, I had years of experience as a manager and business owner. I was Regional Sales Vice President for Mark-Kay Plastics in Kansas City, Missouri; co-founder and executive Vice President of Leffer Systems of New Jersey, a manufacturing company; and International Manager of Technology for Brockway, Inc., a *Fortune 200* company. I also co-owned and operated a retail business.

I am a registered professional engineer, six-sigma black belt, certified project management professional, co-author of *Creating In-house Sales Training and Development Programs*, author of *Unlocking Lean Six Sigma*, as well as a host of other education and training materials.

I would enjoy hearing from you and finding out how this book has helped you achieve your goals. Please contact me at wdonahue@centrestar.com

Best wishes for your continued success.